In the Age of the
Real-Time Enterprise

Oliver Wight Publications, Inc.

EXECUTIVE BREAKTHROUGH SERIES

Breakthrough Partnering: Creating a
Collective Enterprise Advantage
by Patricia E. Moody

In the Age of the Real-Time Enterprise
by Tom Gunn

InfoPartnering: Using Quick Response to
Create Ultimate Customer Delight
by Andre J. Martin

The Innovation Edge: Creating Strategic
Breakthroughs Using the Voice of the
Customer
by William Barnard and Thomas F. Wallace

**Planning & Control in the Age of Lean
Production** by Darryl V. Landvater
(Available April 1995)

Recreating the Workplace: The Pathway
to High Performance Work Systems
by Steven R. Rayner

Reengineering: Leveraging the Power of
Integrated Product Development
by V. Daniel Hunt

In the Age of the Real-Time Enterprise

**Managing for Winning
Business Performance with
Enterprise Logistics Management**

THOMAS G. GUNN

omneo

An imprint of Oliver Wight Publications, Inc.
85 Allen Martin Drive
Essex Junction, VT 05452

I dedicate this book to my wife, Sandra.
Loyal supporter, highly knowledgeable of
business, and my most perceptive critic—
without her encouragement, hard work, and
sound advice, this book would not have
been possible.

Copyright © 1994 by Thomas G. Gunn
Published by Oliver Wight Publications, Inc.

Oliver Wight Publications books may be purchased for
educational, business, or sales promotional use. For
information, please call or write: Special Sales Department,
Oliver Wight Publications, Inc., 85 Allen Martin Drive, Essex
Junction, VT 05452. Telephone: (800) 343-0625 or
(802) 878-8161; FAX: (802) 878-3384.

Library of Congress Catalog Card Number: 93-060671

ISBN: 0-939246-43-0

Printed on acid-free paper.

Manufactured in the United States of America.

10 9 8 7 6 5 4 3 2 1

Contents

List of Exhibits

In the Age of the
Real-Time Enterprise

Introduction

Xerox Corporation reduces inventory by one-third, or $650 million, and reduces supply chain cost by another $150 million while customer satisfaction increases. Digital Equipment Corporation reduces inventory over $700 million. Sun Microsystems Computer Corporation reduces manufacturing cycle time from 280 to 175 days, freeing up $1.2 billion in cash. Wal-Mart stores have only 40 percent of the inventory storage space of their competitors. And store sales of 7-Eleven Japan are 30 percent above their closest competitor. In addition, the company enjoys an operating margin double that of the same competitor.

North America's leading manufacturers—*all* its major computer companies, Deere & Company, Caterpillar, Northern Telecom, General Electric, Sikorsky Aircraft, Pratt & Whitney, the Trane Company, Pitney Bowes, and others—are replanning their manufacturing operations in minutes to an hour, rather than in six to forty hours.

Compaq Computer Corporation saves over $50 million in three and one-half years using an advanced manufacturing planning tool. Deere & Company reduces its dealer restocking order-to-delivery cycle 60 percent, from twelve weeks to five using the same new tool.

Xerox Corporation creates the position of corporate vice president, integrated supply chain, reporting directly to its chairman and CEO.

United Parcel Service invests more than $2 billion in modern information systems over the past six years.

In the retailing business, a major revolution is in the making as power shifts from manufacturers to retailers and the final consumer.

In 1993, Pittiglio, Rabin, Todd & McGrath, a respected high technology consulting firm conducted a bench-marking study of how effectively manufacturers produced and delivered their products. Their first kind of manufac-turer produced and sold systems, typified by a mainframe computer and its many peripherals. Their second kind of manufacturer produced and sold commodity goods, such as power hand tools found in consumer product stores.

First, they reported the time required for each type of manufacturer to plan, make or source, and deliver its goods as follows.

	DAYS BEST-IN-CLASS	DAYS AVERAGE
Systems	166	267
Commodity	76	170

Then they reported in the same manner on the perfor-mance of dozens of surveyed companies against several other important performance factors.

Total logistics cost as a percent of sales:

	BEST-IN-CLASS	AVERAGE
Systems	6.7%	14.5%
Commodity	4.8%	12.7%

Cash-to-cash cycle:
(Calendar days)

	BEST-IN-CLASS	AVERAGE
Systems	63	124
Commodity	33	118

Percent orders shipped on the customers' requested date:

	BEST-IN-CLASS	AVERAGE
Systems	87.2%	59.1%
Commodity	99.0%	72.5%

Value-added per employee:
(US$ × 1000)

	BEST-IN-CLASS	AVERAGE
Systems	142.2	99.4
Commodity	171.4	104.0

How can even the average players compete against this kind of operating supremacy, much less those companies below average?[1]

WHAT IS GOING ON HERE?

The companies cited earlier are leaders in implementing a new vision, a way to manage the world of logistics so that they can win in today's intensely competitive global marketplace. They are doing these things at the corporate level, for that is how they are measured in terms of marketplace image, and by Wall Street. They are implementing enterprise logistics management (ELM), a holistic approach to managing their manufacturing operations and their value-added pipeline or total supply chain—from suppliers to final customers.

That they are able to implement this new ELM concept at a corporate level is due to the power of today's information systems, which can track and manipulate huge sets of data on a real-time basis. They can prepare new plans with production data in minutes, not hours or days. They can communicate, either within the corporation or with its external business partners—customers, suppliers, or information utilities—at the speed of light.

Why is it so important for all manufacturers to implement ELM? Because leaders in business understand the truth of the following observation by Peter Drucker, and recognize the urgent need to capitalize on it: "The economy is changing structure. From being organized around the flow of things and the flow of money, it is becoming organized around the flow of information."[2]

In this economy, information—the most accurate, the most rich, and the most real-time—will be the key to global competitive advantage.

Manufacturing is being transformed rapidly from a make-to-stock to a make-to-order business in which a customer order triggers both the design (or final form) of the specific product as well as the production and delivery schedule.

ELM is the next step in more sophisticated management of a vital part of today's manufacturing business. It is essential in the transformation of the *art* of management to the *science* of management so that better business performance will result. ELM is a vision for the global, integrated, real-time enterprise logistics management that is crucial for any manufacturer to survive, grow, and prosper.

This book is organized so that people with different interests and backgrounds can start in different places. Senior management might want to start with chapter 8 before going on to chapter 6 and the other chapters.

Materials management and production scheduling people might find reading the book from the beginning more interesting, if only because they are likely to identify strongly with the material found in chapter 1. Those managers or practitioners highly experienced in the use of manufacturing resource planning (MRP) and (JIT) might start with chapters 4 and 5 to obtain a new perspective before reading the rest of the book. The information systems professional probably will want to start with chapters 7 and 8 before covering the rest of the material.

Enterprise logistics management is here today in concept and in reality in some leading manufacturing companies. It's critically important for each reader to fit his or her company's business under the ELM vision and work with a sense of urgency to implement their company's version of ELM. All other things being equal, competitive supremacy and the greatest customer satisfaction will come to those companies that can operate soonest and most completely in the ELM manner. Get started now. Good luck.

CHAPTER **1**

Enterprise Logistics Management: Today's Reality

FIVE CASE EXAMPLES

The CEO of a $600 million manufacturing company assembled his entire staff on a Friday afternoon for an emergency meeting. He was not a happy person. In a terse voice, he outlined the problems that were crippling his company's performance. On the one hand, he was receiving several phone calls a week from cherished customers berating his company's delivery performance as being unreliable and slow. On the other hand, many key suppliers were calling to complain that the company continually jerked them around with order quantity and delivery date changes. Internally, he pointed out that their own performance indicators showed that a lot of things were wrong—high inventory and overhead, excessive overtime and freight premiums, and low productivity and return on assets. He also pointed out the high frustration level of the company's employees due to their inability to resolve these problems.

They needed to fudge their numbers and work around the company's "systems" to accomplish *any* results. Sound like an unusual company? Not so.

The reality of logistics management is that senior management, as well as logistics management, in many corporations does not have the accurate and timely information it needs to manage its business so that it performs in a world-class manner *and* gives its customers the kind of service they desire. This is true at an aggregate functional level as well as at a detailed product level. It is especially true in large global corporations. Consider the following five, unfortunately typical, scenarios.

Case 1

It is not uncommon to go to a company's senior management meeting where a particular product or product line is being discussed and find that *no one* has all the necessary information or correct numbers in a consistent format on a timely basis for the product in question.

Here's the usual situation concerning any one product. The inventory management people have the figures from last Saturday (Sunday's computer run), but today is Thursday, and they are not sure what has transpired since. Moreover, they are a bit concerned because they cannot find 100 units of this product that the inventory management records show to be in the overstock section of the warehouse. In addition, due to an unusual amount of warehouse activity and overtime, they are afraid that all the inventory movement won't be able to be entered into the computer system in time for Saturday night's weekly update run.

Purchasing has scheduled materials and components due in monthly time buckets and they're not sure how many units have been received or shipped from the supplier yet, or even that the supplier will ship them all in time for them to arrive this month. Worse yet, they have no supplier rating system that automatically rates all suppliers' performances with regard to quality, cost, delivery reliability and lead times, supplier design capability and involvement, and business history, to ensure that only the best companies end up as suppliers for any given item. Purchasing has been having trouble getting accurate requirements from production to place orders in a reasonable lead time with their suppliers, since their manufacturing resource planning (MRP) program is run only on the weekend and many unusual requirements come up in between MRP replanning runs.

The sales forecast for the product in question is for the quarter, and there is a $50 million difference between the unit and dollar forecast for the quarter. This is not considered abnormal, but a bigger problem may be that the forecast hasn't been updated for nine weeks and market conditions seem to have changed dramatically.

The production schedule is in weekly time buckets, and shows past due on several products. The production planners haven't rescheduled this past due in a month because they don't think it's particularly important and, besides, they "hope to catch up soon." The production manager has to have a reasonably accurate sales forecast for this product for the next nine months to see if more tooling needs to be ordered and more assembly workers hired for a couple of hot new products.

Production, too, is concerned about inventory accuracy. The plant's inventory is only "four wall" (i.e., only locates material inside the building, not by area within the building) because there is no accurate and timely shop floor material tracking system to track the flow of material through the lengthy production process. There is an urgent request in to the head of manufacturing to hire three more material control people to join the seven current people whose daily job it is to find and expedite the flow of material on the shop floor. The vice president of manufacturing doesn't understand why anyone would want a computer system to perform material tracking when it's so easy for someone to just ask the machinists where the material is. "People give us the flexibility to adapt quickly," he says.

Sales demand for the product arrives daily, but its input into the company's order entry system often occurs days after the customer places the order. In part, this is due to the bottleneck at the sales department's single fax machine and line. Even more frustrating is the delay in interpreting and keypunching the faxed customer order data into the company's order entry system.

There are supposed to be hundreds of this specific product's units in finished goods inventory, but a lot of the company's customers are not getting their shipments on time. The company lacks a finished goods allocation system, which means the same products keep getting sold to many customers but delivered to only a few of them. In addition, the order-picking people in the warehouse are running about one day behind in filling orders because the warehouse is poorly organized. The warehouse supervisor is told repeatedly that the company can't afford the additional six people he says he needs to catch up.

The company's biggest customer wants 300 units of a particular product delivered a month from today. His sales rep has promised he'll get them this time, but no one really knows for sure if he will. The last time this customer ordered and was promised 200, he received only 120 because the inventory was sold to someone else who ordered *after* he did. So, this time, just to be sure he gets 200 units, the customer is ordering 300.

Finance would like a reasonably accurate projection of sales, inventory, and production over the next six months to see if the company will make its financial projections for the year. In particular, finance is also concerned about the rapidly mounting overhead costs in the entire logistics function—from its distribution warehouses through its production scheduling and material control department, including the procurement function. The CFO can't understand why manufacturing needs so many people and keeps talking about what other companies have achieved with "downsizing."

Everyone in the meeting has his or her own set of numbers to defend and often try to shift the blame to some other department or person, or even to the customers or suppliers. Tempers flare. Political posturing is rampant. Arguments abound in increasingly loud and insulting language. The real problems are (and remain) hidden. Sound familiar?

Management is flying blind in this environment, and the customers (those that are still there!) are suffering for it. Of course, the company's *performance* is suffering the most. These general circumstances are all too familiar to people involved in today's manufacturing environment.

Case 2

It's Monday morning. ABC Manufacturing Company's customer service department has an emergency request from one of its best customers to supply them with 1,000 units of a popular stock keeping unit (SKU) at their standard price by Friday. The company does not have an on-line real-time master production schedule that would show an "available to promise" number that could instantly respond to the customer's request. The customer service rep, therefore, who has jotted the relevant order information on a scratch pad, has to tell the customer he will get back to them as soon (within twenty-four hours) as he can call the plant and talk with all the people who should have input into the answer. Thus, ABC Manufacturing has already failed its customer by not having a reliable answer immediately and by taking a day out of the customer's decision time.

The customer service rep tries calling four key people in the plant who can get the necessary information and make a firm commitment. He reaches none of them. One is out sick, one is in a training class, and the other two are tied up in meetings. Finally, by the next afternoon, customer service has received enough information from the plant to call the customer and say that they will not be able to handle that large a quantity by Friday. The customer is now doubly upset because they have wasted over a day in getting this supplier's (negative) answer. The customer says they will have to go to another supplier who can deliver an equivalent substitute in time, but at a slightly higher price.

ABC's management has been wondering why productivity is so low in their customer service department. Their analysis shows that on the average, each customer service rep is handling only one order every hour. Management also can't understand why the company never seems to have enough production capacity. But their customer service rep, unable to turn the customer request into an order, often throws the scrap of paper on which the order information is written into the wastebasket. Thus, the company never sees all its demand; it just records sales (shipments) as demand.

Case 3

Because of the demise of a competitor, Nugget Manufacturing Company finds itself unable to satisfy worldwide demand for one of the products it now produces in three of its global plants. It has been a week since this problem came to light, and still no one has the answers to the following simple questions: How many production machines do we have around the world that can make this particular product? How many sets of tooling do we have, where are they, and which specific production machines will each set of tooling fit? What is the condition of the tooling? Is it up-to-date with the latest engineering change? Can it produce products with a Cpk (a measure of specification width to process capability) of at least 2—that is, with world-class "six sigma" quality? Who is the supplier of the tooling and how long did it take to make the last two sets of this specific tooling? Since these questions cannot be answered, a chance for Nugget to maintain or gain market share may be lost.

Furthermore, Nugget may need to ask even more questions. Who are the top 20 percent of our customers, and what has been our record of service to them over the past twelve months? Are we past due on any orders for them now? What is our record of on-time shipment to their first order date desired? What level of back orders are we carrying for them, or what has been our stockout history with their orders? How many times have we been unable to accommodate their order requests? How much business have we lost from them in the past year, and for what reasons?

Case 4

Bitbyte Computer Company can configure, assemble, test, and ship one of its computers in one day. But it takes them a week to create the master production schedule that drives their plant and its supplier network. They can execute faster than they can plan! If this gap between planning and execution continues, it is doubtful that Bitbyte can continue to compete in global markets.

Case 5

Global Manufacturing Company has over 150 plants around the world, many of which supply each other. Because most of their plants' MRP systems replan once a week (on the weekend), it takes several weeks to pass any one assembly plant's requirements through its chain of suppliers in a succession of weekend MRP replanning runs to find out if the supplier plants—internal and external—can handle the assembly plant's demands. By the time an assembly plant finds out that some of its suppliers cannot meet their demand, it's too late. The plant is already one to three weeks into its production schedule and is either dipping into the huge reserves of safety stock it carries or is expediting shipments from another poorer-quality or higher-cost supplier it maintains for such emergencies. No one knows how efficiently and effectively the entire value-added industry supply chain could operate if planning and feedback were possible on a more real-time basis.

WHAT'S WRONG WITH THIS PICTURE?

That there's a better way to run a manufacturing business than the scenarios discussed suggest seems obvious, even to the most casual student of business. Yet, it's worth highlighting the major problems and their high-level causes before we consider the solutions in the chapters to come. Consider three symptoms of the underlying problems.

First and foremost, each of these companies has or will

have *unhappy customers*. No company can survive, grow, and prosper for very long with unhappy customers.

Second, each company's business performance is mediocre at best, and probably sliding toward even lower levels. This will not engender good feelings with the company's investors or with the *new* customers the company is hoping to win.

Third, employees of these companies cannot be very happy. They are clearly not part of a winning team. Furthermore, they're tired—emotionally and physically—from overwork. They have frayed tempers from being told they must work *still harder* to produce better results.

But, on a more fundamental level, the following are common problems these companies face:

- There is a lack of a *vision* of how the logistics business processes should be managed and operated on an enterprise-wide basis.
- No *one* person is in charge organizationally to see that the logistics business processes are optimized within the enterprise and with customers and suppliers for the sake of its performance, and for customer satisfaction.
- There is no long-term plan to improve the company's business performance and customer satisfaction by improving the performance of the enterprise's logistics business processes.
- There is a lack of corporate-wide data definition, including a common vocabulary for employees to utilize in managing the logistics operations.
- There is a lack of common and integrated computer-based application systems to manage the company's logistics business processes that have the following characteristics:

- Common time buckets that standardize planning and reporting periods, at a maximum, on days rather than weeks, months, or quarters;
- Real-timeness in both the display of data or information, as well as in the ability to replan; and
- Feedback information so that progress against a plan can be assessed and the plan adjusted if something is awry.

- There is a lack of appropriate and uniform enterprise-wide performance measures that relate to customer satisfaction and world-class business performance.
- There is a lack of educated, trained, and professionally qualified managers and personnel to manage the enterprise's logistics business processes.

Manufacturers simply cannot compete with these glaring deficiencies today. Other companies around the globe, with more knowledge, with more ambition and will to win, and with more perseverance to manage themselves more effectively, will dominate any manufacturer who persists in not overcoming these problems.

CHAPTER 2

Enterprise Logistics Management: What Is It?

START WITH THE RIGHT PERSPECTIVE

It is vital to start with the right perspective when contemplating the challenge of effectively managing today's global enterprise. To do so, consider the manufacturing business vision pictured in exhibit 2.1.

Relating to enterprise logistics management (ELM), the key item to note on the manufacturing business vision is the value-added pipeline that extends from the enterprise's global customers back through the responsive enterprise to the enterprise's global suppliers. It is through this pipeline that an enterprise sources supplies (materials, components, or information), adds value to them, and ships them in the form of products and services to its global customers.

Most manufacturing companies today are beginning to see the value and necessity of integrating their enterprise globally. In doing this, they ensure that all the company's business processes are conducted in a tightly coupled,

EXHIBIT 2.1: EDS's Manufacturing Business Vision

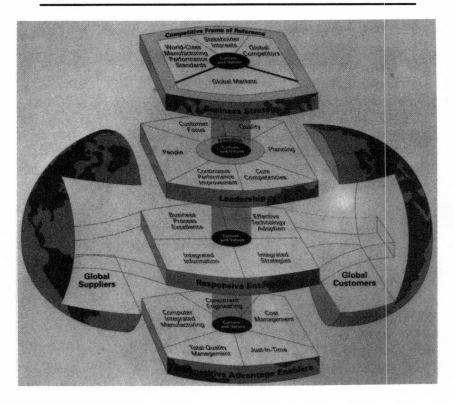

waste-free manner with a minimum of data redundancy regardless of geographical and organizational separation. In addition, leading companies are going beyond this concept of global integration to electronically integrate their enterprises forward with their customers and backward with their suppliers. These corporations are among the first to be able to "plug and play" in the enormous global electronic business network that is being formed today.

The entire framework for ELM centers around the effective management of this global and enterprise-wide value-added pipeline.

In further exploring ELM, we will deal specifically with the competitive advantage enablers shown in the bottom level of the manufacturing business vision. Through computer integrated manufacturing (CIM), we will be integrating the enterprise with modern information systems. Through just-in-time (JIT) principles, we will be eliminating waste in all forms throughout the value-added pipeline and in our management efforts. Through total quality management (TQM), we will put the customer first and focus on managing a zero defect set of business and manufacturing processes. Through modern cost management, especially activity-based costing (ABC), we will know where and when each step in our business processes adds value. In addition, ABC will tell us specifically which customers and suppliers are the most valuable to deal with. Each one of these high-level enablers will contribute to the overall goal of effective and efficient ELM.

ENTERPRISE LOGISTICS MANAGEMENT DEFINED

Clearly, the ELM concept and resulting management system are meant to be applied on an enterprise-wide basis. "Enterprise," as used here, means the entirety of the manufacturing company or corporation. Thus, for global organizations, ELM is a global management concept.

The term "logistics" conveys the idea that ELM deals with the entire materials management and production scheduling spectrum throughout the entire value-added pipeline from final customer/consumer all the way back to the supplier of the "rawest" material. Thus, ELM is concerned with the sourcing and distribution, movement, and storage of materials and products from earliest supplier right through production and distribution to the end user, including any service or replacement parts, or even including gathering products and properly dispersing materials for a demanufacturing/reclamation activity.

"Management" means that ELM is concerned with both the planning and execution activities in a manufacturing enterprise. The problem with some MRP vendors' or industry analysts' use of the term "enterprise resource planning (ERP)" is that effective *planning* only represents *half* the challenge. Timely and faithful *execution* of the plan and the monitoring of performance results represent the other half of the challenge.

While the ELM acronym doesn't specifically say it, another concept implicit in the ELM definition is "integrated." Not only is the approach to ELM integrated in a conceptual sense (spanning the enterprise regardless of organizational and geographical boundaries *and* spanning the entire value-added pipeline), but the resulting ELM *system* eventually will be fully integrated as well.

In a similar sense, a significant aspect of ELM systems will be their "real-timeness." That is to say, data and information will flow on a real-time basis in a modern on-line computer system. This does not mean the kind of real-time response one would find in a process control system where millisecond response or faster is the norm. But neither does it operate as many of today's systems do—in overnight batch mode, or several batch updates a day, or in replanning computer runs that require some six to forty hours or more. By real time, I mean data or information flow that reflects transactions in a few seconds, and replanning runs that deliver answers in less than an hour at worst and in the blink of the eye (or computer screen) at best. Complementing this system of "real-timeness," the just-in-time theme is a fundamental backbone of ELM thinking.

Thus, ELM describes a holistic management system, conceptually and in a computer integrated sense, that spans the enterprise's entire logistics activities—with its customers, within its global "four walls," and with all of its suppliers. Exhibit 2.2 illustrates some of the complexity of the ELM environment.

This is the structure of a large global manufacturing company. Typically, there are several layers of organizational hierarchy. There are also several patterns of manufacturing plants—most drawing some of their supplies from external suppliers, and some established to feed their output to other plants in the same organization. All these form the enterprise link in the supplier-to-customer value-added pipeline. Then, in most organizations, this picture becomes even more complex because there can be an entire network of distribution centers interwoven into the picture. Thus, ELM deals with an extremely complex network of organizational, geographic, material flow, and scheduling dynamics. Today, we can begin to think about it as one integrated operating system largely because of the progress we have made in information technology, product design, inventory management, and customer service over the last decade.

ELM represents a confluence of ideas that originated in many different aspects of business. The concepts of MRP and distribution resource planning (DRP) provide a solid base for tying together dependent demand throughout the entire value-added pipeline. The concept of JIT (minimizing waste) and, on a broader front, business process reengineering (BPR) forms the basis for minimizing lead times and inventory throughout the entire value-added pipeline.

EXHIBIT 2.2: The Enterprise Logistics Planning Environment

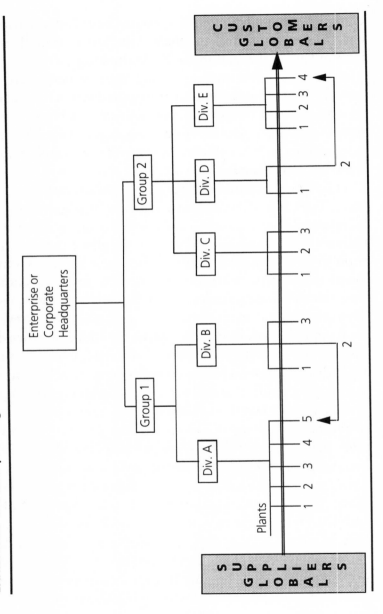

An intense focus on providing customer satisfaction first is an underlying theme of ELM. The concept of customer demand pull and resulting replenishment originated in the grocery supermarket and retailing industries in companies like Wal-Mart, replacing traditional promotional push by manufacturers. Modern information systems—both application software and database management systems—and telecommunication networks make possible the real-time integration of customer-enterprise-supplier hierarchies on a global basis. Better simulation software, particularly based on industrial dynamics modeling, gives us deeper insight into the behavior of complex multilevel distributed systems.

More educated and sophisticated users and executives are responding to a vision that says that the enterprise's logistics and its associated relationships with customers and suppliers *can* be managed as a system, efficiently, effectively, and *cost effectively.* Ultimately, of course, it is competitive pressure from intense global business competition that will continue to drive the concept and reality of ELM into every industry worldwide.

ELM IN CONTRAST TO TODAY'S MRP ENVIRONMENT

Exhibit 2.3 shows some of the functional characteristics of ELM in contrast to today's autonomous MRP systems in most manufacturing organizations.

EXHIBIT 2.3: Old-Think Logistics Versus Enterprise Logistics Management

EACH PLANT AUTONOMOUS	WITH ENTERPRISE LOGISTICS MANAGEMENT
MRP	
Each plant has its own.	All plants materials management/ logistics systems integrated in one common system.
DRP	
Optional, seldom used.	DRP part of integrated system for distribution-intensive products.
Information to/from Corporate	
P&L summary only to corporate from plants.	All plant, supplier, customer information flow available electronically to corporate. All order entry and scheduling information flows from corporate to plants.
Logistics Staff	
Full complement needed at each plant, including purchasing—each plant does its own staffing and training with little or no regard for corporate welfare.	Minimal staffing at plants, main strength at corporate level—all staffing and training done with a consistent approach; the goal is to maximize corporate strength.
Suppliers	
Each supplier services each plant separately; thus, has to deal with a number of customers in the corporation.	Suppliers deal with corporate on aggregated major product purchases, lesser buying done locally, suppliers have to deal with fewer customers and can be more effective for the corporation.

EXHIBIT 2.3 (*continued*)

EACH PLANT AUTONOMOUS	WITH ENTERPRISE LOGISTICS MANAGEMENT

Material Tracking Throughout the Logistics Pipeline

Each plant does its own in different ways to a different extent.	All material movement tracked fully on a common computer system, including use of electronic data interchange (EDI), throughout the logistics pipeline.

Capacity Management

Each plant does its own with little or no regard for corporate performance.	Performed centrally (first) with regard to maximizing corporate performance, then plant performance.

Inventory Management

Each plant does its own with little or no regard for corporate performance.	Performed centrally (first) with regard to maximizing corporate performance, then plant performance.

Customers

Managed by each plant separately and to varying degrees of customer satisfaction, with little or no regard for overall corporate customer priorities.	Managed with regard to overall corporate priorities—strategic and operational.

(*continued*)

EXHIBIT 2.3 (*continued*)

EACH PLANT AUTONOMOUS	WITH ENTERPRISE LOGISTICS MANAGEMENT

Information Systems

Each plant has its own— electronic communication between plants difficult and costly and usually nonexistent, plant to corporate telecommunication usually primitive. Even aggregation of data from separate plant systems difficult due to different definitions, MRP system use, and timing cutoffs.	Corporate systems use standard data dictionary, database management systems, operating system, application system (ELM), and telecommunication system to create and effectively use management information.

Ability to Exchange Design (Geometric) Data Between Plants

Limited to none; each plant may have its own CAD system; plant to plant telecommunications usually nonexistent or primitive.	Full corporate engineering network with sufficient graphics capacity running standard CAD/CAE applications available at all plants.

Types of MRP Systems

Completely separate and different MRP systems for make-to-stock, make-to-order, and process manufacturing.	One core MRP application system with different "flavors" for different manufactured products and processes.

ELM'S UNDERLYING INFORMATION SYSTEMS CHARACTERISTICS

At least two information industry research companies have attempted to focus manufacturers' attention on ELM by developing a description of ELM systems that is almost exclusively information technology based, rather than functionally based. This is of limited use when someone is trying to establish what ELM systems *do,* and how they compare to what's available today. However, we should note these information technology characteristics because they do help flesh out the entire picture.

Most information technology-based descriptions of ELM systems state that the systems exhibit the following characteristics:

• They are based on distributed open systems or, in today's jargon, "client server" architecture. This is in marked contrast to yesterday's MRP systems that were mainframe or minicomputer-based on proprietary computing architectures, or to stand-alone microcomputer-based (e.g., the personal computer) systems.

• They are based on distributed relational database technology. This means the database software must support multiple copies of a production database that are transparent to the user anywhere around the globe. In addition, database access would be through "standard" structured query language (SQL) inquiries. Furthermore, the database management software should be an integrated design with the application software (e.g., MRP, DRP, order entry, procurement, etc.).

■ They are based on fourth-generation (4GL) software code. This is in contrast to the third-generation languages like COBOL used to program older MRP systems. Some have proposed that ELM systems be based on object-oriented programming (OOP), but this remains a "nice to have but not necessary" feature, and one that remains several years away for most vendors' systems.

■ They possess a graphical user interface (GUI). A GUI is the interface the computer terminal user sees and interacts with in utilizing an application program. GUI refers to an icon-based "point and click" screen design as initially popularized by Apple's Macintosh. This is in contrast to the character-based screen that has been the mainstay of the computer user's world for decades. GUI's have the benefit of requiring much less training for the user to become proficient, and they have been shown to greatly increase user productivity over their predecessors.

■ They are enterprise-wide, and support multiplant global operations. In addition, these ELM systems continue their integration with accounting and finance as exhibited by today's top integrated MRP software packages, and would continue this integration push to other vital functions within the enterprise such as product and process engineering or even R&D in some industries.

THE BENEFITS OF ELM

Having gained a general idea of ELM—what it is and what some of its technical underpinnings are—it might make sense to consider what benefits would accrue to the enterprise that has the vision and courage to implement ELM.

First, by being able to perform ELM on a real-time basis,

days and weeks will be taken out of most companies' planning and execution cycles. Thus, ELM-based companies will be more responsive to their customers. But, just as important, *time is money!* Shorter lead times will allow inventory to be taken out of the value-added pipeline at every point. (This is because safety stock is proportional to the square root of lead time for a given service level and variability of lead time.) Removing inventory will free up working capital to be used for other purposes such as R&D, capital equipment or information system investment, employee education and training, and so forth. In addition, any time inventory is reduced, the amount of space and equipment required to keep and manage it is reduced commensurately, whether on the shop floor or in warehouses. Shorter lead times also allow us to reduce the forecasting time horizon, automatically improving the accuracy of the forecast.

Second, being able to plan and react to changing business conditions more quickly will mean *better customer satisfaction.* This is especially important in this age of increasingly volatile global business conditions and JIT thinking. This will have an especially large impact on companies that have a deep supply hierarchy (a long and complex supply chain) or that are themselves toward the bottom of an industry value chain.

Third, manufacturing corporations practicing ELM will be able to *maximize the performance of the corporation as a whole,* rather than just the performance of any one plant or division at the expense of others. Today, in many large corporations, it's frequently each plant (or plant manager) for itself, a fact of life that often encourages gamesmanship in logistics management. While very large and diverse corporations may not choose to manage themselves as one business unit, it is clear that they will have the option and need to manage their logistics performance at some level (e.g., group or division) higher than the individual plant level.

Fourth, *employee productivity will increase* throughout the entire value-added pipeline, since the cadre of expediters and material handlers now needed to locate and track materials and manage huge safety stocks of material will be markedly reduced, if not altogether eliminated. Higher productivity will result in lower costs and/or higher profits throughout the value chain.

Fifth, *senior management will have a much greater awareness of the impact of ELM decisions* because they will have much more information available to manage their business on a timely basis. They will have a choice of graphically summarized information, or if they choose (and are computer proficient), they can "drill down" to any level of detail regarding relevant information they desire on a real-time on-line basis.

Sixth, *management will be able to manage global capacity more effectively*, thus maximizing return on investment, whether that return reflects investments in plant, equipment, tooling, or people.

Finally, *education and training costs will be lower and the degree of operating professionalism will be higher* when a manufacturer's logistics business processes are standardized and are all operated by one common system in one common manner.

As we have seen, and will note more specifically later, the benefits of ELM are significant. Even in a generic sense, they form a compelling reason to implement ELM in any manufacturing company regardless of size. For once any one company in an industry has implemented ELM, then the other companies in that industry need to implement it, if only to achieve competitive parity.

CHAPTER **3**

Reengineering the Five Basic Business Processes

IDENTIFYING MANUFACTURING'S FIVE BASIC BUSINESS PROCESSES

In his book *Process Innovation,* Thomas H. Davenport shows the results of several prominent global companies with regard to characterizing their key business processes. In the table reprinted as exhibit 3.1, we see that IBM arrived at eighteen basic business processes, Xerox at fourteen, and British Telecom at fifteen. Only British Telecom's makes any reference to planning (the business) as a business process.[1]

Hewlett-Packard lists three critical "metaprocesses" that characterize a typical manufacturing organization: "the product management process; the demand management process; and the supply management process."[2]

As a prelude to discussing business process reengineering, let's look at five basic business processes in which a manufacturer must excel. These are:

1. New product and process design;
2. Customer order to delivery;

EXHIBIT 3.1: Key Business Processes of Leading Companies

IBM	Xerox	British Telecom
Market information capture	Customer engagement	Direct business
Market selection	Inventory management and logistics	Plan business
Requirements	Product design and engineering	Develop processes
Development of hardware	Product maintenance	Manage process operation
Development of software	Technology management	Provide personnel support
Development of services	Production and operations management	Market products and services
Production	Market management	Provide customer service
Customer fulfillment	Supplier management	Manage products and services
Customer relationship	Information management	Provide consultancy services
Service Customer feedback	Business management Human resource management	Plan the network Operate the network
Marketing	Leased and capital asset management	Provide support services
Solution integration	Legal	Manage information resource
Financial analysis Plan integration Accounting Human resources IT infrastructure	Financial management	Manage finance Provide technical R&D

From *Process Innovation* by Thomas H. Davenport. Used by permission.

3. Materials management (including production scheduling);
4. Contracting: for defense contractors (with the U.S. government, or any other country's government); and
5. Estimating: for engineer-to-order manufacturers.

The customer order to delivery and materials management business processes can be combined to form the complete logistics business process, but let's deal with these subjects separately, as the former has an external and forward-looking (customer) focus while the latter has an internal and backward-looking supplier focus. These key processes constitute the heart of any manufacturing company's operations.

Recently, I have identified a critical sixth business process that needs to be added to the all-important five above. *Planning* is a business process, whether we are focusing on the strategic planning or information system planning process, or on operations planning. We ought to be able to apply the same principles of business process reengineering to the planning process that are applied to the other five, so that we reduce the time it takes to plan, improve the quality of the plan, lower the cost of planning, and establish a smoother flow of the right data or information into, through, and out of the planning process.

Our focus here is on the entire spectrum of operations planning. This runs the gamut from addressing the question of "Given our current and anticipated products, markets, and sources of supply, how many plants and distribution centers should we have five years from now and where should they be located?" to "What product are we going to make in this plant on each line in each work center on which machine in the next hour?"

DEFINING OPERATIONS PLANNING AND MANAGEMENT

Operations planning focuses on the following subjects:

1. Capacity management. There are three major areas in which a manufacturing company has to manage capacity carefully. The first of these is *facilities* capacity. This involves extracting the greatest capacity from a given set of facilities (including offices), thus helping to ensure superb return on assets for a company.

The second area in which capacity management counts is with production machinery and tooling. Here, the more critical concern is to ensure that an enterprise has adequate capacity *where* and *when* it is needed in order to maximize customer satisfaction at minimum expense and with the least amount of lead time.

Many companies whose capacity is primarily tooling dependent—i.e., companies that use molds, dies, and patterns—fail to recognize the importance of leading-edge tooling management systems to their overall business performance. In many such companies, the *product* management systems are far more state-of-the-art than the *tooling* management systems. Yet, the company may have a higher investment in tooling inventory than product inventory, and the tooling is often the controlling factor in establishing a company's manufacturing capacity and/or short-term capability to satisfy its customers.

Can your company's tooling information management system answer the following questions on an on-line real-time global basis:

- How many sets of tooling do we have for this product and where are they (which plants around the world and where in the plant, or at what subcontractor's location for repair or modification)?

- What is the product or process engineering revision level for each tooling set?
- Which tooling is ready for use?
- What specific production machines will each tooling set fit without modification? (Note that this requires an accurate database of production machinery.)
- What is the status of each tool (ready for immediate use, needs minor repair, needs engineering change update, or needs major overhaul)? How many times has each tool been utilized since its last major overhaul (number of "hits" for a die, number of mold fills, etc.)?
- If ready for immediate use, what is the Cpk value of the last run of parts that came out of the tooling (it must be 2.0 or above for world-class quality)?

Most company's tooling management cannot answer the *first* of these questions, much less a majority of them, and certainly not all of them.

The traditional approach to capacity management has been that of finding and eliminating bottlenecks that place serious limits on customer satisfaction and revenues. But, in a recent article, Esther Dyson suggests that manufacturers could take a different view of capacity and sell it as an expendable entity per unit of time just as the airlines sell their seats.[3] (We'll explore this idea further in chapter 8.) Thus, the challenge here, in order to maximize return on assets, would be how to obtain the maximum amount of revenue for every possible minute of production capacity in a plant. Currently, few corporations have the information needed to accomplish this, but they can still get started toward this vision today.

The third and most traditional area of capacity management is, of course, that of managing labor capacity. This will become even more critical as job skills broaden and manufacturing companies move farther toward a seven-days-a-week, twenty-four-hours-a-day utilization of their plants to maximize return on assets and justify the high level of capital spending on modern manufacturing and information technology in each plant. In addition, companies must consider the high level of spending on the ongoing education and training of all employees.

2. Production scheduling. Traditionally a difficult task, this area is becoming even more challenging as customers demand better service, JIT and EDI (electronic data interchange) proliferate throughout the supply chain, and there is greater pressure on manufacturers to lower costs.

3. Customer order to delivery. This entails all aspects of the "order to cash" business process. Because customers place a high priority on when they receive a product, but not when they pay for it, to stay customer-focused, it is better to stick with the order to delivery term for this business process. The process starts the instant the customer places an order by whatever medium—order to a salesperson, mail-in, phone, fax, or computer to computer by EDI. It ends when the customer has received the order, with 100 percent quality, with each line item filled at exactly the quantity specified, at exactly the agreed-upon price, and exactly when (and not too far before) the customer *originally* wanted the product.

4. Material management. This, of course, covers all aspects of the supply chain or value-added pipeline, from global sourcing to material management within the enterprise to global distribution of the finished product.

Thus, operations planning (and execution) cover the great majority of a manufacturer's day-to-day activities. It plays a major role in determining the business performance of the enterprise and the satisfaction of the enterprise's customers.

TODAY'S OPERATIONS PLANNING PROBLEMS

At the highest level, manufacturing companies often suffer from one or more of the following four problems regarding operations planning.

1. In some companies, *there is no formal, disciplined, proven planning process in use at all.* These are the companies in which planning is relegated to budgeting, and is usually run by the financial organization. In addition, in many such companies, there is an aversion to any other kind of planning. Usually, these companies have a "macho anti-planning culture" in which the emphasis is on action— or, rather, *reaction.* In such companies, costs are high, customers usually have an excessive dissatisfaction level, suppliers are being jerked around constantly, and the human stress and burnout factor produces low morale and undesired turnover.

2. In other companies, *"great plans" are created by staff organizations, but these plans are usually not fully implemented or sometimes even brushed aside by line operating groups.* The reasons for this impasse are that these staff-created plans are too idealistic, or too simplistic, or just never have the buy-in of the operating groups, since they gave little or no input to the process of creating them.

3. In many companies, *plans under consideration or in use have huge dollar/unit gaps because the company is not being driven by one set of numbers, or because it lacks a common planning database and set of operating definitions.* In one manufacturing company I worked with, it was not uncommon to see a $200 million to $300 million gap between the billion-dollar quarterly sales and marketing plan in dollars and the manufacturing plan in units. These gaps make realistic planning impossible and inevitably lead to chaos at the end of the planning time period. Overall company performance and customer satisfaction suffer as a result of these poor plans.

4. Finally, in almost all corporations, *the planning process simply takes too long.* The entire roll-up of the forecast, the gathering and dissemination of data, the endless negotiation and argument over numbers and (real or imagined) implications—whether financial or operational—of various scenarios may take weeks or months to execute. All this is in contrast to many leading companies that have made good progress on reducing lead times in their operations to the point at which they can build and ship a product in two or three days instead of two or three weeks or months. In many companies today, it takes a week or more to create a master production schedule for a product that can be built and shipped in one or two days! Worse yet, customer, shop floor, or supplier changes cannot be evaluated with regard to their impact on the organization until the next time the planning system (usually an MRP system) is "run"—often the following weekend.

REENGINEERING THE OPERATIONS PLANNING BUSINESS PROCESS

Given that some leading companies have been successful in applying business process reengineering to the other more recognized business processes we mentioned earlier, it would thus seem logical and beneficial if we applied business process reengineering principles to the operations planning process. Business process reengineering has been described in detail in my previous book and many other books and articles.[4] The key principles are outlined here.

In business process reengineering, we must first understand the current business process, especially through the eyes of the customer, as the product flows through the business process, with regard to four factors:

- Cost and value-added buildup;
- Elapsed time;
- Quality, or yield—the converse of process loss; and
- The flow of data or information that is required or generated by the business process.

Once the current process is understood in this context, it can then be simplified and the waste eliminated from it. The focus of the reengineering activity should be to answer the following three questions:

1. Is this work necessary?
2. Does this work add value for the customer?
3. If we were to start with a clean sheet of paper, would we do it this way today?

Business process engineering can have a huge improvement impact even if a business uses no computers in its operations at all. But, today, it would be folly to stop short of using modern information technology to enhance each of the organization's business processes. Indeed, it is modern information technology that enables us to perform today's business processes with increased speed, higher quality, greater productivity, and greater flexibility. In addition, we can use modern information systems to integrate the global enterprise itself, as well as integrate it within its global business environment.

THE IMPORTANCE OF QUALITY IN MANUFACTURING AND OPERATIONS PLANNING

Many organizations perceive that they are drowning in a sea of scheduling problems, when really those scheduling problems are only the symptoms of a far more pernicious *quality* problem, not only with the company's products but with its business processes as well.

How can you accurately schedule a plant when you never know when you are going to produce a good part? This is reflected in the popular use of scrap factors in the lot-sizing algorithm of most MRP systems today. For example, if the scrap factor is 10 percent and the lot size is 100, 110 units will be started in production, *hoping* to net 100 good-quality products.

How can you operate with maximum manufacturing efficiency if the error rate in taking customer orders is in the 5,000-occurrences-per-million-orders range, or about 2.8 sigma quality—hardly the 6.0 sigma necessary for world-class quality.

Exhibit 3.2 demonstrates the long march toward world class quality. Many North American and European manu-

EXHIBIT 3.2: The Journey to World-Class Quality

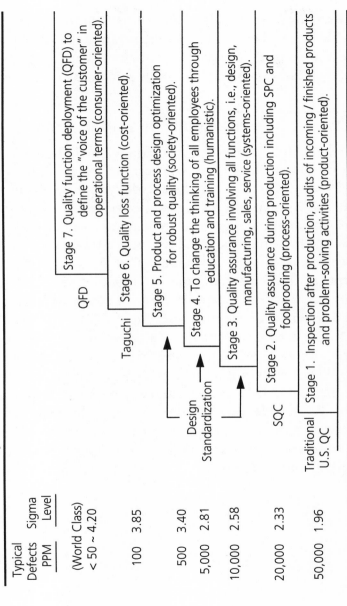

Typical Defects PPM	Sigma Level		
(World Class) < 50 ~ 4.20		QFD	Stage 7. Quality function deployment (QFD) to define the "voice of the customer" in operational terms (consumer-oriented).
100	3.85		Stage 6. Quality loss function (cost-oriented).
		Taguchi	Stage 5. Product and process design optimization for robust quality (society-oriented).
500	3.40		Stage 4. To change the thinking of all employees through education and training (humanistic).
5,000	2.81	Design Standardization	Stage 3. Quality assurance involving all functions, i.e., design, manufacturing, sales, service (systems-oriented).
10,000	2.58		Stage 2. Quality assurance during production including SPC and foolproofing (process-oriented).
20,000	2.33	SQC	Stage 1. Inspection after production, audits of incoming / finished products and problem-solving activities (product-oriented).
50,000	1.96	Traditional U.S. QC	

Adapted from: L. P. Sullivan, "The Seven Stages of Company-Wide Quality Control," *Quality Progress*, May 1986.

facturers are currently still at Stage 1 or 2 in this diagram. To what extent they solve their quality problems will determine the relative ease with which their scheduling and capacity utilization problems can be resolved.

THE PATH TO INCREASED BUSINESS PERFORMANCE

It seems obvious that most corporations could make major progress toward higher business performance goals if they could measurably improve their underlying business processes and combine excellence in operations planning with increased enterprise logistics system integration. The result of doing this would be a greater understanding of their current capacity and capabilities. The flip side of these benefits is that the corporation would also understand its current capacity and capability *shortfalls* and be able to remedy them in an organized manner.

Planting a seed for chapters to come on the value of information systems, we close this chapter on business process excellence by noting what Ray Stata, president and CEO of Analog Devices, Inc., said in a recent letter to the editors of the *Harvard Business Review:* "Business processes define the ways people interact as well as the *information content* [italics mine] of these interactions to achieve intended results."[5]

CHAPTER 4

Understanding Today's Manufacturing Planning and Control Systems

IDENTIFYING THE TWO MAJOR ASPECTS OF MANUFACTURING PLANNING AND CONTROL SYSTEMS

In order to gain a sound understanding of manufacturing planning and control systems, it's important to realize that there are total quality management, computer integrated manufacturing, just-in-time, and cost management aspects of manufacturing planning and control systems.[1] We will focus particularly on the CIM and JIT aspects of manufacturing planning and control systems, shown in exhibit 4.1, because these two subjects may not be well understood by senior management, particularly with regard to the effective integration of them to serve a highly complex, discrete product-manufacturing environment. Then we will move to a discussion of the inadequacies of these systems in

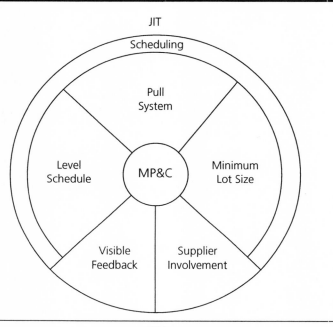

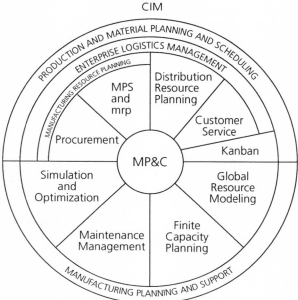

today's and tomorrow's business environment, and also identify the barriers to the implementation of the ELM solution in manufacturing companies today.

Manufacturing planning and control systems play a vital role in determining how effectively a manufacturing company performs because they cover the entire logistics spectrum from procurement to production to distribution and after-sale customer support. They thus play a critical role in a company's performance of the two logistics business processes—the customer order to delivery process and the materials management/production scheduling process. In addition, they serve as the foundation for much of the operations planning business process.

Their traditional roles cover materials management (purchasing, inventory control, and distribution) and production scheduling. Recently, with the advent of the MRP II concept, such software systems also include integrated accounting and finance applications. As such, they represent major business application systems that cut across a majority of any manufacturer's activities. In terms of sophistication, manufacturing planning and control systems run the gamut from simple two-bin inventory management systems, neither paper- nor computer-based, to computer-based manufacturing and distribution resource planning (MRP and DRP) software packages.

THE FUNCTIONAL GROWTH OF MANUFACTURING RESOURCE PLANNING

As a first step toward understanding today's manufacturing planning and control systems, consider the growth of MRP systems over the last twenty-five years. Exhibit 4.2 shows the growth in functionality of MRP systems since their

EXHIBIT 4.2: MRP—More Functional Integration[2]

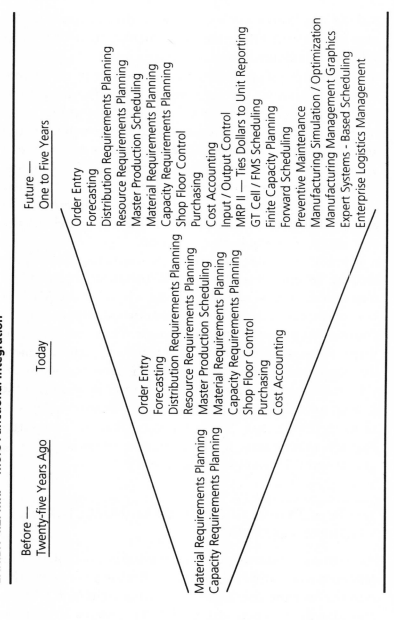

Before — Twenty-five Years Ago	Today	Future — One to Five Years
Material Requirements Planning	Order Entry	Order Entry
Capacity Requirements Planning	Forecasting	Forecasting
	Distribution Requirements Planning	Distribution Requirements Planning
	Resource Requirements Planning	Resource Requirements Planning
	Master Production Scheduling	Master Production Scheduling
	Material Requirements Planning	Material Requirements Planning
	Capacity Requirements Planning	Capacity Requirements Planning
	Shop Floor Control	Shop Floor Control
	Purchasing	Purchasing
	Cost Accounting	Cost Accounting
		Input / Output Control
		MRP II — Ties Dollars to Unit Reporting
		GT Cell / FMS Scheduling
		Finite Capacity Planning
		Forward Scheduling
		Preventive Maintenance
		Manufacturing Simulation / Optimization
		Manufacturing Management Graphics
		Expert Systems - Based Scheduling
		Enterprise Logistics Management

inception in the late 1960s and their expected growth in the near future.

When MRP was first being developed in the late 1960s by people such as Ollie Wight and Joe Orlicky, and by IBM with its PICS software package, it was called "material requirements planning" (now called "mrp"—"little MRP"). In those days, mrp consisted of two primary software modules that ran in a batch mode: material requirements planning and (infinite) capacity requirements planning. Over the next twenty years and two to three generations of software, functionality (including more on-line capability) was added in software modules until the average MRP package sold today generally contains, at a minimum, the functionality for manufacturing shown in the middle column of exhibit 4.2. (Note that all aspects of procurement systems are included under MRP.)

As more functionality was added, the name evolved into the broader term of "manufacturing resource planning." When accounting and financial applications were added to the overall package, the name was changed to "MRP II" to indicate the package's even broader overall capability. (We'll continue to use the term "MRP" as a descriptor for all MRP II systems.) During these twenty-five years, software packages were developed to run on all three CPU sizes—mainframes, minis, and micros (personal computers or workstations)—under many different operating systems, and in conjunction with many different database management systems.

Where are these systems going in the future? For part of the answer, see the right column of exhibit 4.2. Additional capability has and will continue to be added in response to growing user sophistication and needs that give MRP software the following capabilities:

■ *Schedule group technology (GT)-based shop floor cells or flexible manufacturing systems.* Here, the MRP netting algorithm would gather all parts with certain GT codes to schedule through one or more of these cells or systems before proceeding to process lower levels in each part's bill of materials.

■ *Perform finite capacity planning.* Some manufacturers built very sophisticated finite capacity planners into their MRP systems as early as the late 1970s. Most of these, though, were disasters when implemented, because the rest of the manufacturing environment was not under sufficient control with regard to quality, master production scheduling, quick setups, lot size reduction, work-in-process tracking, data accuracy, and the education and training of their people. As a result, most of these finite capacity planners just pushed work out on the time horizon to reflect an overloaded master production schedule, overly long lead times, and priorities within the finite capacity planner that *all* were in the highest 2 percent to 5 percent of their priority range.

Today, there are some finite capacity planners or schedulers being sold, usually to be used as a separate unintegrated adjunct to MRP. They have had modest to good success in the very few plants that are sufficiently sophisticated to use them.

While the designers of these in-house MRP systems with finite capacity planning capability were theoretically correct, the rest of the company wasn't ready for this level of sophistication. Indeed, few are even today! As a result, most early finite capacity planners were unplugged and the plant went back to operating with infinite capacity planning or no capacity planning at all without much degradation in performance.

- *Perform forward as well as backward scheduling.* This capability is an important part of building more simulation capability into MRP software. The algorithm is the same as backward scheduling, only the starting point is different— today (or any day), instead of the customer due date.

- *Provide an integrated preventive maintenance (PM) capability.* Most preventive maintenance software sold today is sold separately from MRP software by separate vendors. This complicates the communication and coordination between MRP and PM. The goal is to have an integrated PM software module in the MRP package that automatically takes a machine out of consideration for scheduling by MRP when it is due to be down for preventive maintenance, or when it is out of commission for unplanned maintenance.

- *Utilize true probability-based simulation,* based on Monte Carlo sampling from known probability distributions. Net change MRP systems provide "either/or" simulation, either condition one or condition two, depending on a human's input of likely conditions or outcomes. Simulation capability could provide the likely outcome of following a specific course of action based on the laws of probability that more closely mirror the real-world manufacturing environment.

- *Utilize true optimization capability with linear programming.* This could be used to establish transportation network models that analyze optimal warehouse locations or on a more frequent basis to select the best shipping carriers and routes for a given set of criteria.

■ *Allow more graphically based reporting,* thus doing away with pages of difficult to read or interpret numbers. MRP output could be summarized in colored, easy-to-interpret graphs whose trends and messages could be understood more quickly by all users, including senior management.

■ *Utilize expert system knowledge (artificial intelligence).* Materials and scheduling experts could build a knowledge base and a set of experience-based rules that could be applied automatically when the MRP system was run for any one part or production facility. In some cases, this might eliminate most of the need for human planners to work daily with the system's output and exception messages. This concept is built into product configurators that front-end some MRP packages for make-to-order manufacturers today.

■ *Allow enterprise level logistics management.* Initially, MRP systems were for single plants and had no DRP capability. Currently, many MRP systems provide multiplant capability and a few have integrated DRP capability. Future MRP systems will have both capabilities and thus could be used at a corporate or group level to provide an overview of that entire business unit's logistics activity from global suppliers through the business unit to global customers.

So the trend in MRP systems is increasing functionality and integration, and there probably will be no letup in this trend for the next decade. The manufacturing press is full of reports of a few sophisticated manufacturers enhancing their MRP systems' functionality. It usually doesn't take more than two to three years for these features to start showing up as features or options in the software packages of most of the leading MRP vendors.

It is interesting to note that the growth of the MRP

software industry has resulted in a diminished *rate* of functionality enhancements in MRP software over the past five years. MRP software vendors have been preoccupied with acquiring other companies in their industry to gain installed base and preempt their competitors. In addition, they have been consumed with the porting of their systems to new platforms either horizontally across a given level (mainframe or, especially, mini) or vertically (from mainframes to minis and then to microcomputers). Now that a greater degree of industry consolidation has occurred, and a "final" solution platform has been identified (a workstation or PC based on DOS or UNIX, Microsoft's Windows NT, or the emerging operating system from Taligent—a joint venture of Apple and IBM), we can expect to see renewed progress toward more functionality and integration in these powerful software packages. In particular, we already see vastly improved user interfaces with the recent advent of graphical user interfaces, or "GUIs," as they are known.

In summarizing the growth of MRP systems, we find that they have been fueled by four main factors:

- The increasing sophistication of users and their demand for even more—and more integrated—functionality;
- The unparalleled rate of progress in information technology, both hardware and software e.g., applications, operating systems, database management systems, and for telecommunications;
- The increasing competitive pressure on both the suppliers of MRP software and all its related information technology components, and on all manufacturers from global competition; and
- The infusion of new ideas from the world of JIT and the OPT philosophy of Eli Goldratt.[3]

Parallel to the growth of MRP, the use of modern technology such as bar codes, radio frequency (or wireless) communication, electronic data interchange (EDI), and satellite tracking has made it feasible and cost-effective to track the flow of materials throughout the entire logistics chain on a "real-time" basis. Today, there are no excuses for losing materials as they flow through a company's supply chain.

THE HISTORICAL IMPLEMENTATION OF MRP

As an aid to understanding how we got to where we are, consider how MRP has been traditionally implemented in most manufacturing companies. It has been, for the most part, a bottom-up approach. Manufacturers first experimented with MRP in one plant. Often this required two or three attempts before they obtained sufficient data accuracy and discipline on the shop floor, had a critical mass of people educated in MRP thinking and modern materials management, and achieved a successful MRP implementation.

Fueled by that learning and the considerable benefits of a successful MRP implementation, MRP then began to spread to other plants within a particular manufacturing company. Finally, when some companies had MRP in every plant, they implemented multiplant MRP to handle situations in which one or more of their plants supplied higher-level fabrication or assembly plants. In this case, MRP would be successively run for the assembly plant and each "level" of plants upstream—fabrication, and perhaps even raw material manufacture—to link the entire manufacturing environment together with all plants driven by a common set of requirements.

In almost all cases, MRP systems were not implemented with any overall corporate plan, either for information systems or for logistics. They also were implemented without any of the business process reengineering that has come to the fore recently. In addition, many manufacturers grew in the 1980s by acquisition, thus further complicating any opportunity for consistency in their approach to MRP system implementation or operation. The result is that few, if any, manufacturers ever designed, successfully implemented, and operated their MRP or logistics system(s) as a total enterprise (corporate) logistics system.

INTEGRATING MRP WITH JUST-IN-TIME THINKING

With some background in MRP established, let's return to a broader discussion of manufacturing planning and control systems by bringing JIT into the picture. Here, we are focusing our application of JIT on the manufacturing planning and control system environment. To do so, let's start with some definitions of commonly used but often misunderstood terms.

Kanban is the information system used to manage JIT production. A kanban or sign can range from a colored golf ball, to a paper or metal sign on the side of a standard material handling container, to a standard material handling container itself, or to a computer-printed and barcoded paper sign on a container.

Kanban is part of JIT production, which is a way to produce the necessary units in exactly the right quantities at the right time. JIT production is in turn a part of a much larger system—the Toyota Production System, initially developed and implemented by Taiichi Ohno and others at Toyota in 1947, and in continual enhancement ever since.

They originally described this system as a way to make products so that costs are reduced, quality is improved, and respect for humanity is enhanced.[4]

Many excellent books and articles have been written about JIT production in the last five to ten years, and we will not discuss those concepts and "how-tos" in this book. JIT is extremely simple conceptually, but has proven to be inordinately difficult to implement in Western societies because it requires new management thinking and practices.

The one aspect of MRP and JIT that I want to explore involves the current "push/pull" thinking about both systems. For the past few years, a number of consultants and college professors have been running around the country telling people that MRP is a failure—it's a "push" system that is inherently bad. On the other hand, JIT is a "pull" system, and that is inherently good—right up there with cleanliness, apple pie, and motherhood. The not too subtle message is: "Throw out MRP *and all those computers*, implement JIT, and all of your troubles will be over." Let's consider the situation more carefully.

While these JIT enthusiasts may paint an extreme picture to make a point, I think this kind of thinking is naïve, simplistic, and, if actually carried out, dangerous for most manufacturers. Every bit of evidence we have shows that business throughout the world is becoming more competitive, more volatile, and more complex to manage due to the production of ever-smaller lot sizes of increasingly differentiated products. Indeed, there is evidence that Toyota, the inventor of the Toyota Production System and one of the world's most sophisticated auto producers, is *adding* inventory buffers in its assembly plants to cope with their product/option proliferation and small lot production.[5]

No one needs a computer, but once one manufacturer

has one, everyone needs one. And thus the race is on. Modern information systems are essential competitive weapons today that deliver the benefits of speed, higher quality, higher productivity, and flexibility to any function or business process.

At the outset, it is important to recognize that JIT has been most successful in repetitive manufacturing—relatively high volume fixed-routing manufacturing. At Toyota and many other places, to be most successful also required that end item demand be smoothed by a large finished goods inventory buffer (or backlog) so that plants could be run at a relatively fixed rate over time—usually with no more than 5 to 10 percent variance in short-term daily master production schedules. We *have* been able to learn a lot of important principles from JIT production that we can apply to all other manufacturing environments. But the primary use of and benefits from JIT production have been in repetitive manufacturing.

Both MRP and JIT are—or can be—pull systems. Final assembly requirements expressed by some form of master production schedule pull products through the factory/ supplier environment. There are those JIT zealots who espouse a true "demand pull system," wherein a customer order immediately triggers a factory order to pull exactly that quantity of parts through the plant. If this is what is desired, all you have to do with an MRP system is to set the finished goods inventory and safety stock levels to zero in the MPS, and the customer order will flow directly through to the factory—*if* you run the MRP system "real-time," or at least every night.

It is no inherent fault of MRP systems that they are push systems today. Instead, manufacturing people make them that way by operating them with a lot of "fat." How?

With regard to lead times, most manufacturers make them too long in purchasing and manufacturing (final assembly and fabrication). If it takes two weeks to get a part from a supplier, we say, "Let's cover our tails and make that four weeks." If final assembly takes one week, we put a two-week lead time into the MRP system for a little protection, thus doubling work in process in final assembly. In a similar manner, most companies insert extra-long queue and move times in each product's routing.

Furthermore, the back-scheduling algorithm in almost all MRP software uses fixed lead times that are lot size independent instead of lot size dependent. At a minimum, this implies a lot of lead time maintenance in the system if your company has a JIT program going and you are concentrating on reducing setups and reducing lot sizes on a continual basis. But, ultimately, you want to be able to produce any required quantity—maybe even as little as one unit—and have the MRP system schedule that properly. For most products, there is a big difference in lead time depending on whether the lot quantity is 1, 100, or 5,000. Try a random sample of ten of each of your company's products to see how lot size dependent their lead times are!

Now consider the netting algorithm that the MRP system uses. First, in the United States, safety stock is typically included as an inventory option. This is our wonderful American just-in-case system—keep some (or sometimes a great deal!) on the shelf just in case!

MRP systems have many lot-sizing algorithm options in addition to lot-for-lot. Lot-for-lot means that if we need ten parts, we only build ten parts—no more or no less. In the United States, most MRP systems are run with economic order quantity (EOQ) lot sizing. At a minimum, this is likely to be wrong because the EOQ formula is based on an assumption of constant demand, and rarely is that the case in manufacturing, especially two or three levels down in the bills of materials.[6] As activity-based costing has shown us, the costs used in the EOQ model are likely to be wrong because of the overhead allocation problems inherent in many companies' standard cost systems.

Then, too, we often use scrap factors in our MRP netting algorithm. The scrap factor reflects the fact that we might have to start 110 units to finally get 100 good ones. The Japanese are amazed by American manufacturers' use of this feature. Their reaction is: "You [Americans] *plan* to build scrap?!" With regard to this practice, note that many manufacturers think that they have a scheduling problem when what they really have is a *quality* problem: they never know *when* or *if* they are going to produce a good-quality part!

Consider a lot-sizing example. We'll leave out the safety stock, as it is the first thing handled by the netting algorithm anyway—and often it is never consumed. Let's assume that in our MRP system, we need 10 parts, the inventory position is zero, the EOQ is 100, and the scrap factor is 10 percent. Thus, we start 110, hoping to net 100. We take our 10, and put the other 90 good parts in inventory. On the other hand, any *well managed* manufacturing operation would start 10 parts, make 10 good parts, not put any units in inventory, and not even need the shelf or inventory space, or stockroom personnel, etc. This represents an entirely new way of thinking for most U.S. manufacturers.

With respect to time buckets, we typically use large ones—quarters, months, or weeks. Why not use days or even shifts? The algorithm is the same and computing power is essentially free today.

Moreover, manufacturers often have inconsistent or untimely feedback from the shop floor vis-à-vis their MRP-generated plan. Often, no material (and/or labor) tracking system is implemented at all, such as a modern bar-code-based system. Manual job tickets may be used, but these are often riddled with human error, or get lost. Even when a bar-code-based material tracking system is installed, often these update the planning database on a batch basis only once or twice a day. This is particularly insufficient in fast-paced manufacturing environments.

Finally, we typically don't replan very often. MRP replanning "runs" are made weekly, every two weeks, monthly, or even quarterly in some companies. One company I visited a while ago ran their MRP system all weekend to produce 16,000 pages of output that had to be analyzed by an army of planners before it could be run again! Oh, suffering horrors! Why not run MRP at least daily, so its output is as close to reality as possible?

Often, companies will run their MRP system in regenerative mode wherein *all* the material requirements are replanned every run, thus insuring the greatest possible replanning run time for any given computer. Many MRP systems can be run in net change mode, in which the only changes made to the plan are a reflection of transactions that have caused changes since the last run.

So the fat creeps in, and a pull system gets changed into a push system. From a scheduling viewpoint, there is little or no difference between MRP and JIT. MRP is a computer-based scheduling and communication system. JIT is most often (here in the United States) a paper-based communication and scheduling system. However, Yamaha's PYMAC system, developed over ten years ago in Japan, is a computer-based combination of a classical MRP system for their job shop production and a single card kanban system for their repetitive manufacturing.[7]

Some MRP suppliers have put JIT or repetitive manufacturing features in their software—features such as rate-based or cum scheduling instead of individual job orders, backflush inventory relief instead of relieving inventory at stockroom withdrawal—but these features do not alter the fundamental concepts just discussed.

TODAY'S MANUFACTURING PLANNING INADEQUACIES

So what's wrong with manufacturing planning as it's practiced in most manufacturing companies?

First, *the process is haphazard and slow,* especially compared with real-world events in which conditions in the marketplace, a manufacturer's shop floor, or with a manufacturer's dozens or hundreds of suppliers change on a minute-by-minute basis. Many manufacturers have made great progress on the execution side of the business. They can now assemble and ship an order in one to three days, rather than the three to ten weeks they might have required previously, with improvements made possible by business process reengineering and JIT. But, in most such companies, it still takes a week or longer to prepare a master production schedule for only one plant, much less for all the enterprise's manufacturing locations.

Second, as we have noted, *the feedback process to the plan may not exist at all, or it may be slow, incomplete, or inaccurate.* Many MRP system implementations lack any material tracking system to show results against the MRP-generated plan. Others may have manually recorded tracking systems with paper tags or tickets that are pulled from shop order forms at every workstation after the work is completed, then are keypunched or scanned into the computer. Even in bar-coded material tracking systems, these are often run in batch mode so that material movement is only updated every night, or every shift, or every few hours.

Third, *it is rare to find that the planning and feedback systems are based on an integrated design using an integrated database and on-line systems.* Too many manufacturers still are stuck with a patchwork of different application systems and hardware that does not communicate effectively or efficiently, that is not user friendly, and often is still run in batch mode every night, weekend, or at month's end.

Finally, *in companies stuck with the kind of MRP systems we have noted, one cycle of the planning effort is exhausting for all the parties concerned.* It takes too long to gather the data, check its accuracy, create the plan, respond to the planner messages, and disseminate the results to all relevant parties. On top of that, some companies are run by myopic managers who are always wondering when their people are going to stop planning and go *do* something! Expedite some parts! Make something happen! Planning, *and disciplined effective execution of the plan* is not valued in such a culture.

When we look at the implications of these planning inadequacies, we find many problems. Because planning manufacturing/distribution operations takes so long and is so involved, there is usually only one plan produced per time period. No one knows if it is the *best* plan, because it is the only one that can be produced. There is no way to know if a better plan by any number of criteria could be produced. Management has never had the luxury of creating *many* plans and *comparing* them to select the best one according to whatever criteria is most important on that occasion—lowest cost, least time, a focus on customer A, doing without all the parts from supplier B, etc.

These problems are only exacerbated in a multiplant production environment where planning for n levels of plants in the supply chain hierarchy generally takes $n-1$ time periods. Consider the following example using the common weekly time buckets and planning run, and assuming a three-level plant hierarchy of only one plant per level. On weekend one, MRP is run for the assembly plant (level one). The assembly plant planners go over their requirements and pass them to the next lower-level plant (level 2) so that on weekend two, their MRP system can be run with fresh requirements from their "customer", i.e. (at a minimum), the level-one assembly plant. Similarly, the second-level plant passes its requirements to the third-level plant for its MRP run on weekend three. Sometime in the first three days of the *third* week, the planners in the level-three plant discover that their plant cannot (in the course of normal events) meet the requirements of the two levels of the plants above. *But* the top-level plant is already two weeks into its schedule, and the second-level plant is already one week into its schedule! It's too late to correctly plan the entire chain of plants so that problems are minimized and customer satisfaction at all levels including the end customer are maximized.

What often happens in these situations is that the "macho managers" in the lower-level plants say, "Don't worry, somehow we'll meet the schedule." The old "can do" attitude, right? And often they do! But *at what cost?* At what cost in overtime, what cost in incoming and outgoing freight premiums, what cost in jerking their suppliers around, and at what cost in human stress and strain! All (or most of) this extra cost and stress could have been avoided if we could have quickly run through several planning scenarios for the entire multiplant chain before any schedules were released.

Ultimately, the implication of the way manufacturing planning and control systems still operate is that the enterprise's logistics performance is poor. The total enterprise suffers from high inventory levels *and* poor customer service. The lead times in its logistics business processes are too long. Costs are too high, especially overhead and facility costs. Worse yet, management lacks sufficient, accurate, and timely information to effectively manage the business in today's fiercely competitive global markets. People continue to work harder, not smarter. The only way out of this situation is to implement a new way of managing the enterprise's logistics activities. This sounds easier than it is, however, for there are many barriers to overcome in order to implement this new enterprise logistics management vision.

BARRIERS TO IMPLEMENTING ENTERPRISE LOGISTICS MANAGEMENT

There are many barriers—both technical and management—in enterprises today to implementing enterprise logistics management. Let's consider the technical ones first.

Most manufacturing enterprises do not have an integrated enterprise-wide manufacturing planning and control system. What they have instead is a hodgepodge of MRP, and maybe DRP, systems in use, and perhaps even some plants that don't have MRP yet! Some of these systems are old, while others are of more recent vintage. Some are integrated packages, while others are based on a patchwork of homegrown code, often written in obsolete programming languages. The enterprise's many MRP systems have different functional capabilities—some have two-level master scheduling capability while others don't; some have full pegging capability while others have no pegging capability at all. Moreover, the enterprise's many different MRP systems often use many different database management systems or file structures. This complicates any attempts at integration or consistent data management. Finally, many manufacturing enterprises do not have the telecommunications infrastructure in place to communicate electronically and perform enterprise logistics management. It is either nonexistent or doesn't connect to all facilities consistently, is too slow to pass the required data, or is too overloaded with E-mail and other applications.

In addition, most enterprises' manufacturing planning and control systems are being *operated inconsistently.* Their MRP and DRP systems are being used with different planning horizons. Some go out two or three years, some only six months. These systems also are being used with different timing cutoffs and/or shop calendars. One plant's week ends on a Friday night, another's on a Saturday night. One plant works a standard four-four-five quarter, another plant uses a different timetable. Then, the many MRP/DRP systems are operated with different-size time buckets. Some of the companies' systems are bucketless and are reporting in daily buckets. Others are being operated with weekly or monthly time buckets. Others use a variety of bucket sizes over their planning horizons. To further complicate things, the multitude of MRP/DRP systems are being operated with a variety of different data definitions. A bolt in one plant is a cap screw in another plant. Some plants' units of measure are in metric units, others are in the English system. The enterprise lacks a common data dictionary for manufacturing, and often for all the other major business functions or processes, too.

Last, each MRP replanning effort—regardless of the combination of MRP system and computer system, or whether regenerative or net change replanning is utilized, or whether run on a mainframe or minicomputer—often requires between four to thirty (or more!) hours of computer time to execute. Not only is each replanning effort costly in terms of computer time, but the implication of this is that MRP replanning has to be done over a weekend. Thus, the enterprise's plants are lucky to get one MRP run per week, *if* the data for each run turn out to be valid, and *if* the job stream doesn't abort at some point, and *if* the computer doesn't go down, and *if* the company doesn't lose electrical power. If any of these events happen, then the MRP run gets done on Monday and Tuesday at the expense of other computer applications and users in the company, or, worse yet, it often gets postponed until the following weekend.

Manufacturing replanning with MRP is seldom possible, on a daily basis (at a minimum), especially across the usual manufacturing enterprise. The manufacturing applications require a disproportionate share of the company's computer time. And in those enterprises with multiplant environments, really useful multiplant or supply chain planning cannot occur.

Formidable as they are, the technical barriers to enterprise resource planning pale before the management ones. A major barrier to enterprise resource planning is that senior management does not understand the potential benefits and technical feasibility of managing logistics in an enterprise-wide manner. Most CEO's don't come from the logistics or even from the manufacturing function. Even if they did, their knowledge of how to manage these areas effectively today may be considerably outdated and riddled with old paradigms.

Second, most corporations currently have a highly decentralized organization structure and operating style that are not supportive of enterprise logistics management. Most corporations have no person or organization to take the lead for conceiving and implementing enterprise logistics management in their operations. The person in charge of information systems can have a major influence on solving many of the technical issues referred to earlier, but those issues are not the most important ones to be remedied. From a management point of view, there is no one responsible for enterprise-wide logistics (the entire spectrum), and no one person to even *sell* the vision to until one gets to the COO or CEO level.

Furthermore, the current organizational incentives may preclude greater corporate performance. In these environments, the focus is on maximizing the performance of each autonomous plant or business unit without explicit concern for maximizing the performance of the enterprise as a whole. Often, each plant manager is rewarded for maximizing the performance of his or her plant, sometimes at the known (or unknown) expense of other plants or business units in the company.

Thus, the barriers to the implementation of enterprise logistics management are substantial in most manufacturing enterprises, whether in the United States, or anywhere else in the world. In later chapters, we'll suggest ways to overcome these barriers so that your company can be among the first in its industry to reap the many benefits of the new and powerful concept of enterprise logistics management.

CHAPTER **5**

Real-Time
Operations Planning

HOW REAL-TIME PLANNING DIFFERS FROM SIMULATION

Real-time replanning, made possible by technical break-throughs in computer hardware and software, opens up a whole new and more sophisticated world of ELM. Consider how the average MRP user has become mired in the tradition of thinking that MRP can only be run once a week, at best! Instead of one replanning run per week or even one per day, several MRP replanning runs can now be made in the course of one-half to two or three hours. Now the capability exists to run MRP on a *comparative* basis, using *production* data to simulate different customer, factory floor, or supplier conditions. Each replanning run can be used to iterate toward an ever more feasible and desirable solution. Although it is unlikely that any single solution presented is an optimal solution in the truest sense of the word, experience shows that the final solution chosen after several MRP replanning runs is generally far better than the one obtained from just blindly following the first MRP run, as most companies have to do today.

Note that the scenario described is different from the

usual simulation exercise. Traditional simulation modeling starts with an *abstraction* of real-world events and data so that the problem can be collapsed to a set that can be easily modeled. Once the simulation is done, its results must be extrapolated back to the real-world environment being modeled.

In contrast, when using real-time MRP, the user is simulating events with *production* data. No abstraction—with its resulting simplification or distortion—is necessary. The data used in the real-time MRP run are real, and the results of the replanning runs can be applied directly to the company's manufacturing environment if so desired.

THE HISTORICAL DEVELOPMENT OF REAL-TIME MRP PLANNING

Real-time MRP replanning was first developed in 1984. Three engineers from Mitel Corporation in Ottawa, Canada, were dissatisfied with the time NCA's MaxCIM MRP software running on the DEC VAX computer available at that time took to regenerate a new plan. They formed a new company called Cadence Computer Corporation, and used new planning algorithms that arranged the data for MRP replanning in a different way. At the same time, they designed a totally new and proprietary parallel architecture computer on which the replanning part of MRP would run. Implementation of this dramatically faster combination of software and hardware began in 1987 at a division of Northern Telecom, and thereafter at premier manufacturing companies such as GE, IBM, AT&T, United Technologies Corporation, Hewlett-Packard, DEC, Deere, Caterpillar, Compaq, and many others. One of the real drawbacks to buying from Cadence in those days was the fact that a manufacturer had to buy this tiny Canadian start-up's parallel architecture computer. The reaction from potential customers was often: "Oh, no, not another kind of proprietary computer" and "How long have you guys been in business [and how much longer will you be]?"

The solution to this dilemma came in the late 1980s, when new, powerful RISC-based workstations such as IBM's RS/6000 and Hewlett-Packard's HP9000/700 became available. These machines were extremely fast, in part due to the massive internal memory with which they could be configured. In addition, they were cheap and could be purchased from the stalwart companies of the computer industry who could offer a full measure of support and future enhancement for their products. The Cadence people thought that run times would be increased when their application was ported to these new RISC machines, but they were not. Replanning on these RISC-based machines was just as fast or faster as when performed on their Cadence parallel architecture machine.

When Cadence wanted to make a more aggressive marketing push into the United States, there was already a U.S. company named Cadence Design Systems, Inc., in the computeraided design business. Thus, they changed their name to Carp Systems International (CSI), which they were known as from 1989 through 1993. In 1994, the company was renamed Enterprise Planning Systems, Inc. (Enterprise).

With the exception of another Canadian company, formerly Monenco, now named AGRA Software, which has only a PC (DOS)-based "quick MRP" package named FastMAN, no other hardware or software vendor as far as we know has developed the same real-time replanning capability as Enterprise.

While Enterprise enjoyed a long monoply on "quick MRP", their strategic window based on fast replanning monopoly would have come to an end perhaps by 1995 or 1996 by brute force from the manufacturers of larger and faster parallel architecture computers than Cadence's small machine as they designed or ported an MRP software package to run on their machines. But "quick MRP" is only a means to an end. However, users' experiences with "quick MRP" products have demonstrated that real-time replanning capability is only the *first* benefit the user gets from the system. Once today's users get used to the real-time replanning capability, they then begin to see many ways to exploit the power of MRP/DRP logic in analyzing various operating scenarios to improve their company's business performance.

THE GENERIC BENEFITS OF REAL-TIME MRP PLANNING

One of the most obvious benefits that accrue to a manufacturer by speeding up the planning process is that they can react more quickly to increasingly volatile business conditions in the global economy. There is no reason why MRP replanning can't be performed on at least a nightly basis in most manufacturing companies. Indeed, there is no reason why MRP can't be run in real-time if appropriate. Most manufacturers will need to gradually evolve to real-time MRP, because jumping in one leap to this would be too bold a step in most cases.

With real-time replanning, the MRP plan can be divided into finer increments. Daily time buckets can be split into daily buckets by shifts, if desirable. Then, too, there is no need for net change MRP anymore. It's just as quick to replan *all* the requirements as only those that have changed over the past time period.

One of the most interesting side benefits of this effortless real-time replanning capability is that the planning for *both materials and labor* can be accomplished in the same quick computer run. In effect, the computer uses bills of materials and routings in a combined *bill of operations* that reflects how the product is actually made. Thus, the user can see the effect of master production schedule inputs on both materials—including their suppliers—as well as labor or machine capacity in their plants simultaneously. This greatly reduces the number of iterations needed to arrive at a feasible or best possible production and procurement plan.

Given the quick replanning capability, *multiple* MRP replanning runs can be routinely made, allowing easy comparisons of the results from each run, resulting in a fine-tuning of manufacturing's response to a given business situation. Lot sizes can be changed. Alternative routings can be tried. Labor can be added or deleted. Overtime can be scheduled. Noncritical work can be moved out. Make/buy decisions can be changed. With real-time MRP, the results of these changes can be seen in minutes.

Pitney Bowes Corporation, a $3.5 billion manufacturer of postal metering equipment, has been using Enterprise's APS since early 1992 to carefully plan and manage capacity in its component fabrication plant that feeds several assembly plants. In their pre-Enterprise environment, a capacity planning run in their ASK ManMan system running on a DEC VAX used to require seventeen to twenty-five hours. Using Enterprise's APS running on a Hewlett-Packard 9000 RISC-based workstation, they get the same capacity planning report in five to six *minutes.*

John O'Connell, a consultant to Pitney Bowes and one of the Pitney Bowes team that implemented APS, points out that APS has been useful in cleaning up the bad data they (like so many other manufacturers) were operating with in earlier years. Now, they routinely answer questions about manufacturing capability in less than an hour. John comments, "We'd stored up a decade of questions to be answered. I don't think anyone [yet] understands the full capability of this system."[1]

John also points out what many other users of this real-time planning capability have found as they gain experience and insight by using the system, namely, that the level of questions they can analyze quickly with the system has gotten more complex as they continue to learn.

Real-time replanning capability can be made to operate with any software vendor's MRP software package, including highly sophisticated MRP systems—or even just bill of material explosion/netting algorithms—that have been developed in-house by some manufacturers.

Many manufacturers with mainframe-based MRP systems are finding that the acquisition of quick MRP replanning capability saves them from an expensive computer hardware upgrade that costs from two to ten times what the quick replanning hardware and software costs, and still won't perform as well. Moreover, this quick replanning capability may extend the life of their current legacy systems, giving them time to plan and move more prudently into the still-evolving world of open distributed ("client server") systems. In addition, because replanning can be done more quickly, computer capacity is freed up for other parts of the company (or other applications) to use. This may allow more software development or maintenance to be performed, or other software applications to be run more frequently.

IS FASTER MRP DESIRABLE?

Some executives have questioned the wisdom of faster MRP from two aspects: first, won't it simply mean faster garbage in and faster garbage out, and, second, won't having this quick replanning capability result in an extremely "nervous" MRP system?

With regard to the first point, yes, quicker MRP will result in producing garbage faster if the fundamental MRP data accuracy and/or user discipline are insufficient. However, those leading-edge manufacturers using such systems and pursuing the ELM vision as an aid to world-class manufacturing performance know this, and have already established the data accuracy and discipline to operate their MRP and DRP systems effectively. Any manufacturer who hasn't done this must first do so before moving to real-time replanning and the much more complex management challenge of ELM.

As a short-term goal, the initial thrust of having the quick MRP replanning is to be able to run MRP at least once every twenty-four-hour period to keep abreast of increasingly volatile business conditions. Leading-edge manufacturers will soon be able to run MRP in real-time mode. How will they handle the resulting potential "nervousness," that is, having requirements constantly changing so they never know what to do? There are several elements in the answer to this question.

First, management will set (and the software will allow the setting of) limits around master production schedule customer order numbers that present "alarms" to planners. Unlike traditional MRP reschedule messages, any orders coming in that book demand beyond practical capacity limits would send the planner a message *before* the MRP replanning.

Second, MRP will be run as a two-stage system, where the on-line system would have the current plan, and a shadow system would run in "background" in simulation mode. Here, the effects of minute-by-minute changes to customer orders, supplier schedule changes, and quality or production problems on the shop floor will be received and calculated. Planner simulation and review would occur before such changes were periodically dumped into the official on-line MRP system.

Third, lead times in MRP systems will be lot-sized dependent, rather than fixed, as they are in most systems today. Furthermore, a key to reducing the ill effects of schedule nervousness for all manufacturers (up and down the total supply chain) is to continue to reduce lead times.

In the all-electronic future, *everyone* will have greater visibility in tomorrow's supply chain. Manufacturers will be more closely coupled (electronically) with their customers and suppliers. Electronic feedback from their shop floor material and quality tracking systems will be more immediate. Forecasts or requirements from sales or customers will be available and updated more frequently. I believe real surprises will occur less frequently in this dynamically balanced value-added pipeline network. When they do occur, simulation through real-time MRP at more than one level in the supply chain will ease the pain of working toward a graceful (least pain for everyone) solution.

On a more philosophical note, more nervousness and its pernicious effects are relative concepts today. We have only some idea of how customers are slaves to their suppliers' MRP systems today relative to what they really want in customer service. Moreover, by following today's relatively frozen schedules, we inevitably build into inventory or ship some products before a specific customer really needs it (often merely to record revenue in a current time period).

In addition, by following today's relatively static assembly schedules without fully understanding their consequences on lower-level plants or suppliers (due to the usual one MRP replan per week limitation of most of today's manufacturers), we often accommodate the final assembly schedule, but the question is: *at what cost?*

The ELM system should reflect the reality of customer demand on a timely basis. Through system features, management policies, and human intervention in exceptional cases, customer order, shop floor, and supplier nervousness can be dampened sufficiently to run manufacturing plants and distribution facilities more efficiently and effectively, with the fullest possible understanding of available options and contingencies.

ADVANCED REAL-TIME MRP PLANNING APPLICATIONS

Whether within one plant, or applied across the enterprise or its supply chain, the *biggest* paybacks from the real-time replanning capability come from the *new* applications that are available or can be quickly developed and implemented in the user's organization. Let's discuss several of these applications.

Drop-In Analysis

For example, a customer calls on Monday with a rush order well inside normal lead time. The request is: "We need one thousand of these products by Friday. Can you do it?"

Normally, with an overnight MRP run, the question couldn't be answered on any factual basis until the next day ("We'll get back to you tomorrow"), and a day of valuable production time is lost in the process. With a weekly MRP run precluding any sophisticated analysis, most plant managers and planners are forced to take their best "SWAG" and try to force a solution, at unknown cost to their employees, suppliers, and perhaps even the customer wanting the order.

With real-time replanning and a drop-in analysis application, several MRP runs can be made quickly to show the true effect of trying to satisfy this customer's need. If the runs show that, for instance, there are 548 parts that have to be produced or procured within lead time, then chances are that even the best of companies working overtime cannot accomplish that in four days, regardless of the consequences to their suppliers or other customers. On the other hand, if there are only twenty-three parts that need to be manufactured within lead time, then not only is there a good chance that it can be accomplished, but the MRP system will show precisely what has to be done to move these twenty-three parts in, and the exact consequences of doing so on other customer orders and work center workloads.

Using a real-time planning system, Compaq Computer was able to add $6 million to its bottom line through the use of drop-in analysis in their second quarter of 1990.

Some companies don't want to hire any more permanent workers on the shop floor. In this case, they could perform drop-in analysis with regard to planning labor capacity and restricting the addition of new employees. MRP could be run many times using various combinations of alternate routings and machine assignments until the goal was either shown to be feasible or not.

Of course, the opposite of drop-in analysis is a sudden customer order cancellation. Here, it's important to be able to understand quickly the impact of a canceled order on capacity, costs, and other customer orders. With real-time replanning, an exact answer can be obtained quickly.

Engineering Change Analysis

Quite often, management can choose when to effect or "cut in" an engineering change that has no legal or safety mandate to be satisfied. Then, the operating question revolves around a compromise between using up all the old design's parts and materials and committing purchasing and inventory holding costs in order to have the new design's materials and parts on hand.

To illustrate the benefits of this application, assume weekly time buckets are being used, and refer to exhibit 5.1. With real-time replanning capability, all that is required is that we set up a "macro" of, for example, ten MRP runs, vary the engineering change cut-in one week at a time, and compare the inventory and procurements costs between the old design's and new design's components. We would get a set of reports and a graphical exhibit such as shown in exhibit 5.1, where there would be a point in the ten weeks at which total costs would be minimized. That point would be the optimum time to effect the engineering change. This is a prime example of the power of real-time replanning and its ability to spawn new and useful applications. This kind of analysis was not practically possible before! How much money could companies save with this one example of analytical power made possible by real-time replanning?

EXHIBIT 5.1: Engineering Change Cut-In Analysis

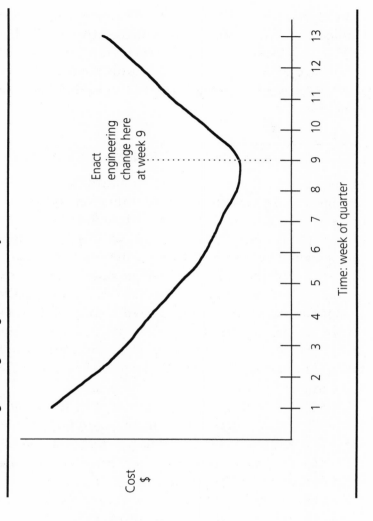

In its very first week of using this new approach, Compaq Computer saved $350,000 in inventory that would have otherwise become obsolete. By their own estimate, they have saved more than $50 million with the use of Enterprise's APS over the three and one-half years they have been using the tool.

LOGISTICS AND MANUFACTURING POLICY ANALYSIS

In this application, the effects of changing different policies relevant to logistics and manufacturing can be assessed quickly. Such policies usually are determined by management without much formal analysis, yet can greatly affect the operating performance of the enterprise. Policies that deal with lead times, lot sizes, safety stocks, setup times, queue and move times, shop calendar and overtime changes, capacity utilization, material costing, and the like can be evaluated. Not only are the implications of such policy changes immediately evident, but also the user can find additional benefits to applying policies in a more differentiated manner instead of across the board.

Deere & Company's production control group in its Waterloo works, working with manufacturing personnel, reduced inventory by 18 percent using a real-time planning system to simulate the effect of policy changes on routings, scrap factors, and order policies.

Can build analysis: Here, the focus is on how to most effectively use up old or excess inventory, while minimizing the purchase of new components and materials.

Common parts analysis: This application highlights component parts that are common among products or product families.

Implosion analysis: Typically, as will be explained in more detail later, planning takes place down a supplier hierarchy. That is, the top-level (usually assembly) plant passes its requirements to its supplier plants, who in turn pass their requirements to their supplier plants, all the way back to raw material suppliers. The philosophy is "Here is what we need to manufacture our master scheduled products." However, the reality of the business world today is that not all manufacturers get what they need when they need it. Sometimes, the reply that comes back up the supply chain is "Here is all you're going to get [or we can possibly give you]."

In this case, the overriding question for the top-level manufacturer is "Given that's all I can get of a particular component, *what's the best mix of product I can build?*" Here, a "reverse MRP" or implosion planning run is needed that shows the answer to this question. Of course, "best" can have a wide variety of criteria. Is "best" that which achieves the greatest revenue for the quarter? Or is "best" that combination of products that produces the greatest measure of customer satisfaction for the order in hand? Or does "best" mean building those products that will result in the least amount of leftover inventory?

Another way of using implosion is to highlight all that could be made in view of a material or component shortage. Thus, the shortfall between that revenue and the planned revenue would provide a framework to evaluate what it would be worth to solve that shortage problem, perhaps by sourcing from a different supplier somewhere else in the world. Then, too, implosion could also be used to answer the shortage question incrementally: "If that's all I can build because of this given component or material constraint, what part will I run into a constraint on *next?*" So implosion gives a manufacturer a newfound ability to work intelligently back up the supply hierarchy to maximize output by a variety of criteria when supply is material constrained for any reason.

In summary, the potential for new applications with real-time replanning capability seems unlimited. An executive at IBM, a longtime user (with a corporate license) of this type of software, once commented that "the use of this [real-time planning] system is limited only by your imagination." Every business is different—in its products, processes, and management strategy and style. No matter how long any company has been using this capability, it will find itself on a continual learning curve of exciting new applications and benefits.

EFFECTIVE SUPPLY CHAIN MANAGEMENT

In the long run, without a doubt the positive effect of real-time replanning capability on any manufacturer's *entire supply chain* will be of the greatest importance to their overall business performance. Primarily, this is because materials account for some 40 percent to 70 percent of most manufacturers' sales dollar, whereas, in contrast, distribution on the other end of the value-added pipeline only averages about 6 percent to 8 percent of their sales dollar.

Almost every manufacturer who is not totally vertically integrated in one facility has a hierarchy of plants—their own, or their suppliers'—that feeds raw materials and components to their highest-level assembly plant(s). The following example of this concept (see exhibit 5.2) uses a three-level hierarchy, but the principle remains the same and the benefits are even greater when there are more levels of supplier plants in the industry value chain or supply chain hierarchy.

In the traditional way things are done today (with weekly

EXHIBIT 5.2: A Typical Supplier Hierarchy

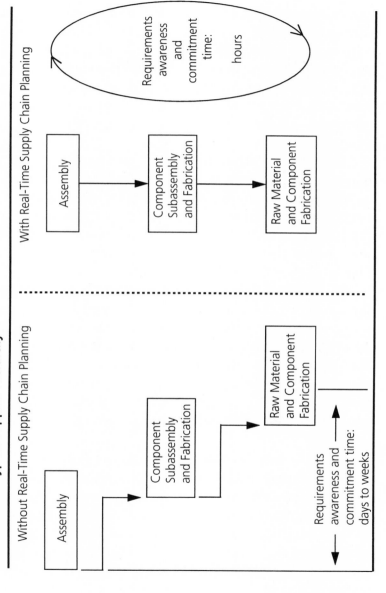

MRP runs over the weekend), the level-one assembly plant runs its MRP over weekend number one and passes on its requirements to its next lower-level plant(s). Often, these requirements are passed computer-to-computer using EDI, or sometimes by fax. But there are still companies that mail their requirements in the form of computer printouts—a process that extends the time frame in this example.

The level-two plant then inputs the level-one plant's requirements, along with those of its other customers, into its master production schedule and runs its MRP replanning calculation on weekend number two. In the same way, the level-three plant runs its MRP system on weekend three, using the level-two plant's (and all its other customers') input.

So, allowing time for planner analysis on Monday through Wednesday of the third week—ten to seventeen possible working days after the level-one plant has its schedule established, management in the level-three plant finds out (at least some percentage of the time) that it cannot satisfy the demand from its higher-level customer(s). But, by then, the higher-level customers are, respectively, more than two weeks and one week into their schedules!

Typically, one of two things happens. (1) The level-three plant people respond by voice and fax and start to work the problem, and arrive at a solution that won't get incorporated into *anyone's* MRP system until the following weekend run. Ideally, the solution would be worked out with the users' slow MRP systems one level at a time, adding at least as many days or weeks to work back up the hierarchy as they required to go down it. (2) The lower-level plant sucks in its gut and, in the great "macho tradition" of manufacturing everywhere, says, "We'll make it happen." Then chaos starts, as existing schedules and priorities get torn up and hastily redone on "hot lists" outside the system, production is rushed—probably compromising quality. All kinds of extra costs are incurred, including overtime and freight premiums, human fatigue and burnout occur. Existing suppliers to the level-three plant are jerked around, and perhaps other customers suffer postponement of their order deliveries. Sometimes, the goal is accomplished, but at what cost? No one can ever quantify the hard costs, much less the more pernicious "soft" costs, relating to customers, suppliers, and employees. At other times, the level-two plant isn't satisfied, and everyone loses.

This example takes into account only the time it takes to make one planning pass down the three-level hierarchy. It still does not consider communication back up the hierarchy and the several planning runs needed perhaps by all participants to *iterate* toward an effective (ideally, the lowest total cost) solution for all participants in the supply chain.

Now adding real-time replanning capability at the level-one assembly plant is of considerable benefit to the users there, as we have pointed out. But that is only a small portion of the possible benefits to be obtained! What good is it to be able to understand the effect of a forecast or customer order change at the assembly level plant by 10:00 A.M. on Monday morning, only to find that when the new requirements are passed to the level-two supplying plant, they won't be able to analyze the effects on their plant (and their suppliers' requirements) until they make their MRP run over the next weekend! This logic follows all the way down the supplying plant hierarchy, whether the plants belong to the manufacturer or to its independent suppliers.

The ultimate benefit from real-time replanning capability will come when *every plant* in the hierarchy has the real-time replanning *and* feedback capability. The key question for today's manufacturers to consider is: How quickly can a change in forecasted or real demand be communicated in specific material and labor requirements all the way down the supply hierarchy and *back to the assembly plant level?* With the combination of real-time replanning capability, EDI, and other forms of networked computer-to-computer communication, the answer for any company should be available in a few hours, not the days, weeks, or months that the current process takes in most manufacturing companies and their internal and external supply chains.

In the future, ELM planning systems will continuously iterate through this supply chain planning cycle. Leading manufacturing companies that use Enterprise's APS, such as GE and Pitney Bowes, are already starting to request that their key suppliers have their own real-time replanning capability (at least for their few products, if they are produced on one line or in one cell) in order to shorten their entire supply chain replanning cycle. The customer's requirements will pull products from the top-level assembly plant, which, in turn, will pull requirements from its supply hierarchy. Multiplant plans will be evaluated and adjusted quickly so that schedules attainable at the lowest total cost are implemented throughout the entire enterprise logistics chain, including the enterprise's suppliers.

TRUE MULTIPLANT MRP

In the past, some manufacturers operated MRP in (their own) multiplant environment where there were interplant orders of parts and materials. In almost all cases, they were handicapped by having to operate MRP for their internal supplier chain of n levels in the sequential cascading manner we described earlier. The output of any single plant's MRP run would be used as input for another plant's MRP run, usually at a later time. As we saw, this leads to a situation in which planning cycles are extended to days or weeks, perhaps even months, depending on the complexity of the supply chain hierarchy.

A very few MRP software packages and sophisticated homegrown systems had true multiplant capability in which there was one common database and application system, so all plants could be loaded into a huge corporate database where every record had a plant code attached to it. Thus, the MRP system could make one pass through the entire database and plan every plant's requirements all in one (long) run. The difficulty with this arrangement was that every plant had to run their MRP the exact way the others did and every plant had to be in precise synchronization with the others. The implementation of such an inflexible system was a nightmare in a large corporation.

Today, it is easier to accommodate the heterogeneous computing environment found in most large corporations and work with distributed data from different plants and even database management systems. Thus, the need for one huge corporate system, operated rigidly to no one's satisfaction, has lessened. In today's distributed MRP system environment, manufacturers can use real-time replanning for multiplant MRP in two ways. They could just operate each plant's MRP system in the sequential cascade faster (in real-time), and there may be corporations where, due to their autonomous cultures, this would be desirable. Or manufacturers could pull in each plant's data (regardless of which MRP system and database management system were used) into a huge central database and make one planning pass through the plant-coded data before distributing it back to each plant. In this scenario, the central database would only be "rolled up" for the purpose of planning and simulation, not necessarily production. In any event, real-time planning capability makes it much more feasible to operate true multiplant MRP planning in a more flexible manner that is more suited to the reality of current manufacturing and information system environments in most corporations.

Real-time replanning capability is a key to shortening the cycle time of the planning business process. Those companies that implement real-time planning capability first will be a long step ahead in achieving competitive advantage in ELM and with their customers.

CHAPTER 6

What's Needed to Implement Enterprise Logistics Management: The Management Factors

We've established the vision of enterprise logistics management as an outgrowth of the opportunity to reengineer today's operations planning business process and gain crucial operating business performance improvements. Current information technology has provided the technical tools that make the ELM concept feasible: the data definition and management capabilities, the telecommunication capabilities, and the ability to perform real-time replanning. Now it is time to turn our attention to the hardest part of the implementation job, the *management* factors that will determine the ultimate success of the implementation and the performance improvement of the business.

GETTING TOP MANAGEMENT INVOLVED

The first task necessary to get started on ELM implementation is to get top management involved. The initial task is to make them aware of the opportunity (need) for improved operations planning as an enterprise, and the feasibility of implementing the vision. This involves convincing them of the very real financial and strategic benefits of ELM for their corporation. Awareness can be generated by an enterprise-wide survey of their current operations planning process and the diversity of systems, capabilities, policies, procedures, and people who play a key role in it. For most corporations, no executive, when presented with such an overview, can avoid coming to the conclusion that there must be a better, lower-cost, more effective way to do things in this area. Such opportunities should, of course, be pointed out in the presentation by the subject matter experts who develop it. The case for change and dramatic improvement will also be reinforced to the extent that the corporation can come up with any benchmarking data on how leading companies or perhaps even competitors perform in this area. One interesting exhibit would be a diagram showing several companies' inventory-to-sales ratio versus their gross margin. Other input to such a presentation could come in the form of comments that result from interviewing key customers and suppliers. Here, the focus would be on customer satisfaction (or the lack thereof) when dealing with the corporation, on their ease of doing business with it, and on the corporation's ability to react to changing business conditions quickly.

It also would be useful to involve the company's senior management in a look toward the future in terms of how they are likely to have to operate in order to survive, grow, and prosper. For instance, I believe that leading large corporations will soon have a senior executive who is in charge of ongoing relations for one or more specific corporate customers around the globe. Suppose you are that executive from Cooper Industries, a Houston-based $6 billion company that has about 160 plants around the world, and that you are in charge of the company's relationship with Ford Motor Company. Ford buys products from many of your plants and divisions, and you are in charge of Ford's customer satisfaction for all of Cooper Industries. What are some of the questions you might naturally seek real-time answers to on a regular basis? How about these for a start?

- How much did Ford buy from Cooper Industries last year in total? How does this break down by division and plant within Ford *and* Cooper Industries?
- How much do we plan to sell to Ford this year? How much do they plan to buy from us this year and for the next three years, again broken down by a plant and division level? Do our expectations match theirs? Have we turned down any Ford business in the past two years because we didn't have the capacity to meet their specific requirements?
- What was our record of delivery to Ford on a plant-by-plant basis with regard to quality, order completeness, and shipping reliability? How do each of our plants and divisions rate in Ford's supplier rating system?
- How are we doing *today* with regard to satisfying Ford's requirements? Are we currently past due on any shipments to Ford?
- Do we have the specific production capacity to handle our anticipated sales on a product and geographic basis to Ford (and our other customers) over the next three to five years?

Few, if any, corporations could answer these questions at a corporate level, especially on a real-time basis and with easily understood graphically based summaries. But these are only a small sample of the kinds of questions whose answers can make a huge difference to customer satisfaction and corporate business performance. Obtaining the right answers to these questions on a timely basis means that substantial improvements are needed to the information system of most corporations as well as to their business strategies and management methods.

Finally, senior management has to be educated as to what other leading-edge corporations are doing in order to improve their business performance by improving their operations planning and execution capabilities. While less than a handful of corporations have the full ELM vision implemented, many companies have already made substantial progress toward this vision.

We learned in the early days of MRP implementation how important top-management understanding and support were to a successful implementation and disciplined use of the system. Michael McGrath and Richard Hoole, writing in the *Harvard Business Review,* amplify this concern when they say: "As our work with Xerox Corporation, Digital Equipment Corporation, Coulter Electronics, and other companies indicates, moving toward global integration is a long, involved process that begins at the top, filters down through the organization, and includes innovations across all functions."[1]

Implementing ELM will be no less difficult than MRP, and will require even more of top management's vision, sponsorship, support, and leadership.

ESTABLISHING THE ELM ORGANIZATION

The second step is to establish the organization that will spearhead the implementation of the corporation's ELM vision. At the outset, this organization will most likely be a small one, whose role will be limited to a staff function. Depending on the size of the enterprise, this group might include only two or three people, or it might range up to ten or twelve.

As for staffing, no less than the company's best people in the field of logistics and information systems will do, no matter what the level of pain and protest of the business units from which they are seconded. This group should contain both former line and staff people—a mix of "old pros" and recently educated "young chargers." It will probably make little difference where they are located geographically in this day of electronic communications such as E-mail and teleconferencing. The arguments to be made in favor of geographical disbursement seem to equal the arguments in favor of co-location of the entire group.

A key question to be addressed is what level of authority this new group should have. Initially, I believe that they should start out as a senior staff organization with no line authority. But clearly, over time, this group could evolve into the enterprise's operations line management group with regard to logistics and operations planning.

One of the key functions of this group will be to work closely over a period of time with its senior management to establish a new enterprise logistics/operations strategy. A vital part of this strategy will be to develop new definitions of autonomy for group, division, and plant-level managers.

A second key task for this group will be for it to establish a corporate budget for implementing the ELM vision. One of the primary deterrents to selling this concept and its associated information systems today is that everyone is afraid it will have to come out of their budget. In other words, just as there is no one in charge of implementing ELM (because the vision doesn't exist in most companies), there is no budget for it either.

Although decentralization has become popular during the last decade or two in manufacturing, we will probably see an increased trend toward centralization. If we give senior management the timely and accurate information they need to effectively manage their companies, once management has such information, no doubt they will see the benefits of centralization and move in that direction of their own volition.

CREATING A LONG-TERM ENTERPRISE LOGISTICS STRATEGY

The third step is the creation of a long-term (at least five-year) logistics strategy for the enterprise. This strategy must have several major attributes and address several major areas, namely:

- It must be customer- and supplier-focused. To attain such focus, there is no better technique than to include key customers and suppliers on the planning team or as a subcommittee of it.
- It must be geared toward maximizing the performance of the enterprise *first,* then each of its business units.
- It must be based upon cross-functional *user* input. To keep the core planning task force small, it may be convenient to set up subcommittees of the planning group to

represent narrow functional or business process issues. The trade-off with regard to planning group size always revolves around ease of scheduling a smaller group and the faster progress that can be made within it. But since the real task is to get *all* employees to change, in some sense, fast progress with a smaller planning group is illusory. There is no one right answer with regard to this issue.

- It must contain an information systems plan as the basis for implementation action. Given that most corporations need to make great progress with the elements of the information systems that we discussed earlier, this part of the overall implementation plan is vital to the success of the program.

- It must allow for the reengineering of the enterprise's logistics business processes, that is, the customer order to delivery and materials management/production scheduling business processes, and, of course, the operations planning business process.

With regard to the customer order to delivery business process, Shapiro, Rangan, and Sviokla provide great perspective in a *Harvard Business Review* article by commenting: "In the course of the order management cycle, every time the order is handled, the customer is handled. Every time the order sits unattended, the customer sits unattended."[2]

One could easily extend this philosophy to the supplier side of the value-added pipeline, also.

- It must have an extensive education and training program designed to facilitate its implementation and smooth operation throughout the enterprise. This program must be designed to address the senior managers of the corporation, as well as the lower-level people in the trenches. The program must focus on teaching *why* such change to ELM is necessary (the education) and *how* new business processes and information systems will work in the future (the training).

Ray Stata, president and CEO of Analog Devices, Inc., puts the value of education and training in perspective when he says, "The rate at which organizations learn may become the only sustainable source of competitive advantage."[3]

Most companies underspend by an order of magnitude on education and training. Motorola spends about $1,200 per employee per year on an education and training program that has returned them $33 for every dollar invested. This seems to be the minimum level of effort required to bring about world-class ELM and business practices. Creating the right workforce depends on three people-based factors: sufficient education and training, establishing the right motivational elements, and empowering people (once a vision, strategy, and structure have been established, and the workers are given the tools to perform their jobs in a world-class manner). Note also that the education and training program cannot be just a one-time effort. It must be ongoing if it is to have any lasting positive effect.

This enterprise logistics strategy starts with rationalizing the corporation's (often haphazardly grown) manufacturing structure with an eye to balancing capacity to reflect today's and tomorrow's markets, and establishing the optimal interplant material flow. McGrath and Hoole point out that "coordinating and simplifying materials flow requires two things: (1) balancing production *vertically* within the production pipeline, from component manufacturing to final assembly; and (2) balancing production *horizontally* between plants that manufacture the same or similar products."[4]

Thus, the enterprise's logistics strategy depends heavily on the manufacturing strategy it has selected. In summary, the long-term logistics strategy must aim for quantum leaps in business performance, to be achieved incrementally.

ESTABLISHING NEW MANAGEMENT OPERATING POLICIES

Next, new management operating policies will need to be thought out and implemented in a carefully sequenced manner. While there are many of these, consider two of the most important.

1. At what level in the corporation will order entry and scheduling be "centered," that is, schedules driven down and reporting sent up the organization. In many cases today, individual plants receive customer orders directly and respond to them independently of any other plant in the organization. Little detailed order information is available to anyone else in the corporation, and sometimes it is not even available to enough people in the plant! In other cases, customer orders come in at a corporate level and are sent out to each plant to be executed. There is no correct answer to this issue that we can apply across the board. The case will vary for every corporation, depending on its mix of products, customers, and distribution channels. A small company whose products are related may choose to take orders in at a corporate level. In more diversified companies, orders many come in at a group or division level, with scheduling driven down to the plant level and

reporting at any level of detail available anywhere above that level. Still other corporations may have plants receive orders directly from their customers, with the plant scheduling itself and all reporting at any level of detail available at higher enterprise levels. This center point will probably climb higher, not lower, in the coming years.

2. How will unit-based sales and marketing forecasts and customer orders become the basis for corporate revenue projection, instead of Wall Street earnings per share "estimates"? Many companies are driven by earnings per share projections today that have no grounding in reality when compared with customer orders. These projections become the basis for budgets that then become the basis for phony forecasts and all kinds of game playing by everybody from sales to operations people throughout the organization. The only things that matter and that can be relied upon are customer orders. They generate unit demand, and the dollars follow the unit demand.

While there's an old joke that forecasting is easy unless it's about the future, McGrath and Hoole note in their superb *Harvard Business Review* article that "the biggest problem many multinationals [all companies?] face is that demand forecasting is a politically charged process."[5]

For top asset management performance, production must be based on actual order rates that consume the forecast. The problem is that many companies don't adjust the forecasts that drive the business frequently enough (or at all) to reflect actual market conditions. Thus, optimistic forecasts (and often a desire to keep the plants operating at full capacity to "absorb overhead") continue to produce product and buy materials that can only go into inventory.

ESTABLISHING CORPORATE-WIDE OPERATING DISCIPLINE AND CONSISTENCY

Finally comes the tough task of establishing enterprise-wide operating discipline and consistency. There are many areas where this will be necessary. Consider only a few of the most important below.

1. Sales and marketing forecasts in units must be developed and regularly updated—at least updated on a monthly, if not weekly, basis. This forecast must then become the basis for the company's operating plan and for its revenue numbers.

There are many ways to improve forecast accuracy, some technical and some having a great deal to do with how the sales force is measured and rewarded. All demand attention as ways to improve the quality of the sales forecast that should, along with the company's existing backlog of orders, drive the enterprise.

Of course, there is no substitute for obtaining sales forecasts or requirements directly from customers as an output of their ELM/MRP/procurement systems through computer-to-computer communication (today called EDI). While these requirements also often change or are wrong, at least one set of filters (the salesperson or sales organization) is removed from the forecasting process, thus decreasing the time needed to generate or update the forecast, as well as increasing the probability of its accuracy.

2. Standard time buckets over some minimum standard planning horizon must be established in the enterprise's ELM/DRP/MRP systems. Each system must, at a minimum, be capable of expressing requirements in no larger than daily time buckets. Tomorrow's "bucketless" systems

will be able to achieve hourly (or less) time bucket distinctions. Planning horizons will differ from company to company, but, at a minimum, we might have a format that looks at the first five weeks out in daily buckets, the rest of the first quarter and the second quarter in weekly buckets, the third quarter in monthly buckets, and the fourth quarter and all succeeding ones in quarterly time buckets. Thus, about sixty time buckets would cover a year on a rolling daily basis.

3. Standard timing cutoffs must be established around the company's work calendar. Thus, all days might end at midnight, all weeks on Saturday at midnight, or whatever.

4. Amazing as it may seem, new corporate standards with regard to the definition of raw material, work-in-process (WIP), and finished goods may need to be implemented. These new standards will help to eliminate game playing between plant managers with interplant shipments and promote better corporate cooperation and asset turn performance. There was, for instance, a case in which plant managers defined one plant's output as their input of raw material! Our working task force changed their definition of *raw material* to that material to which the *corporation* has added no value. Finished goods were ready for immediate shipment to the customer with no further work necessary but bulk packaging and labeling. WIP was newly defined as anything in between raw material and finished goods. This put a new corporate emphasis on minimizing lead times and WIP, which in turn resulted in many beneficial manufacturing process (from plant to plant) and plant rationalization changes.

5. Product structure taxonomies may need to be standardized, particularly in companies that have grown by

acquisition. This refers to the hierarchical grouping of products by stock keeping units (SKUs), then into larger groups such as family, group, product line, etc.

6. Real-time feedback to the planning process (necessary for closed loop control in the control engineers' lexicon) may need to be established in three areas—the feedback from sourcing, your company's shop floor(s), and from distribution. As we saw earlier, many companies have no feedback to the plan visible, others have some feedback that is updated in a batch process, often not more frequently than once a day. The technology exists today on a cost-effective basis to get real-time.

7. In the same light as above, perhaps in conjunction with it, real-time event-driven EDI becomes beneficial. Today, many companies are using mailbox-based EDI systems—often from a third party—that are only updated once a day (generally during the night). The AIAG-based EDI systems used in the auto industry operate by polling every fifteen minutes. This should be a minimum for your operations.

8. Real-time tooling management systems need to be implemented to manage the nonproduct inventory of tooling that is so critical for your enterprise's effective capacity management and customer satisfaction.

9. Currency and language conversion routines may need to be built into the corporate information systems to facilitate easy use and quick reporting of business conditions. Language is less of a problem since the common business language of the world is English. However, shop floor workers in other countries *or* here in the United States may not necessarily be fluent in English. Thus, some parts of the ELM system may need language conversion options.

10. Products must be designed for flexible manufacturing and packaging. Here, the goal is to have global core product platforms that facilitate a wide variety of configurations and support an assemble and package-to-order order fulfillment.

11. Senior management must establish customer service level and inventory level objectives. These may vary by class of customer or product or distribution channel.

12. Management must develop and implement a quality program to achieve world-class quality levels with regard to all products and business processes. This will go a long way toward eliminating uncertainty in the operations environment, thus ensuring more reliable schedules, lower cost, and shorter lead time operations.

13. Finally, corporate-wide standard performance measures must be implemented with regard to the performance of the entire value-added pipeline or supply chain, and with regard to ensuring the highest customer satisfaction. There are several tasks necessary in this area, namely:

- Facts must become the basis of performance measurement and decision making. In most companies, the data required for analysis and measurement are either missing completely, or are not sufficiently accurate. For instance, does your company have a statistical record of its supplier delivery lead times, that is, each suppliers' lead time mean (days), and accompanying standard deviation? These data are critical for better supplier management and manufacturing planning.
- The culture has to be changed. Bob Malchione, writing in *Industry Week,* gives one notable example: "Backlog is a time-honored measure of a company's strength. . . .

But high backlog also means slow response to customers. So if you are serious about responsiveness, don't reward backlog. Reward throughput."[6]

- Performance measures generally have to become more externally focused, rather than internally focused. Of course, getting them customer-focused is the first goal. Relating them to other companies in other industries by benchmarking exercises is another aspect of the needed external focus.

The goal is to install performance measures that *pull* the enterprise in a JIT sense toward world-class performance.

What's Needed to Implement Enterprise Logistics Management: The Technical Factors

ESTABLISHING THE RIGHT CORPORATE-WIDE INFORMATION SYSTEMS

From a technical viewpoint, the major underpinning of any company's business performance from now on will be the extent and sophistication of its information systems. Certainly, they are the very foundation of ELM. At the outset, the right enterprise-wide information systems need to be established. This means implementing the following five elements:

1. The enterprise's global telecommunications infrastructure. This includes not only providing the capability for the company to communicate within its global facilities and people, but also the linkages forward to customers and back to suppliers (suppliers of information as well as materials) so that the enterprise can "plug and play" in the emerging global electronic business environment.

2. Consistent and correct data definition on an enterprise-wide basis.

3. Data management systems that can effectively manage globally distributed data. Today's relational database management systems are fast approaching this capability, with the entire world of object-oriented programming and data management just around the corner.

4. Modern computer hardware, appropriately "right-sized" for each corporate business unit in view of its growth plans.

5. Modern applications systems such as ELM (based on MRP/DRP systems).

ESTABLISHING THE GLOBAL TELECOMMUNICATIONS NETWORK

The enterprise's telecommunications network serves as the facilitator of the ELM system. At a minimum, the goal here is to link electronically every corporate facility so that communication within the enterprise can be real-time. In addition, as we have noted, there is a bigger job to be done to extend this electronic communication capability forward to customers and back to suppliers.

There are many strategies that can be used to establish this global computing network, ranging from doing the entire project yourself to purchasing some or all of the telecommunications capability from third-party suppliers. Whatever telecommunications system you establish, you must consider the following three points:

1. The system must have sufficient bandwidth to cover all anticipated network volume and ensure speedy

communication. This is particularly important when graphical data (such as geometric representations of product designs or "drawings") are to be conveyed on the network along with ordinary alphanumeric business data found in sales and marketing, accounting, and ELM systems.

2. The network must be extremely reliable, with alternate network configuration possible to work around any portion of the everyday network that might suffer from degradation or outright failure.

3. The network must be flexible and easily reconfigured to add or delete nodes represented by suppliers, plants or other company facilities, or customers.

Texas Instruments, a $7.5 billion Dallas semiconductor and electronics company, has one of the world's leading-edge telecommunication networks. Some of its characteristics—including how TI uses EDI—are shown in exhibit 7.1.

In speaking of the benefits this network brings to TI, one of their executives noted:

> The network ties employees in a seamless global web, enabling TI to coordinate the scheduling, designing, manufacturing, and shipping of customer orders as if it were a single centralized operation instead of a patchwork of distant business centers . . . the network is absolutely critical for TI to operate on a global basis.[1]

Another major benefit of such global telecommunication networks involves their role in integrating and leveraging the company's employees. A former employee of Digital Equipment Corporation (DEC) was reflecting on the value

EXHIBIT 7.1: Texas Instrument's Information Network

TI ~ $7.4 Billion,   ~ 60,000 employees

- 89,000 workstations / terminals in 340 sites (44 manufacturing) in 30 countries

  - 17 mainframes in two U.S. data centers; average 99.64 percent uptime, subsecond response time.

  - 8.4 million transactions daily, standard applications throughout the company.

  - Another 0.9 million E-mail transactions per day — within seconds anywhere.

- Electronic data interchange (EDI)

  - 2,000 EDI transactions per day with 1,700 trading partners in 30 countries.

  - More than 50 types of EDI documents, EDI transactions go directly to 20 business applications.

  - > 65% orders to suppliers handled by EDI; > 30% of all supplier orders handled without human intervention; > 50% orders from customers are by EDI of DEC's network. When he worked there, DEC's network was comprised of about 100,000 workstations linking their employees and facilities around the world. He noted that whenever he had a problem, all he had to do was to describe the problem on his workstation and send a request for help out on the network. Within minutes, suggestions would start to appear from around the globe, and they would continue to trickle in for days. This is a major but often overlooked benefit of these networks, and perhaps their most important one, ultimately, because they leverage the intellectual capital of the enterprise—fostering the growth of employee knowledge and becoming the glue that binds the enterprise's employees together in an intellectual or even a cultural or spiritual sense.

ESTABLISHING CORPORATE-WIDE DATA DEFINITIONS

Few corporations have their business data consistently defined across the corporation's operating units. A common bolt might be called a bolt in one plant or division, a capscrew in another, and a threaded fastener in yet another. Units of measure might be metric in one group of plants and identified by the English system in others. Part numbering systems differ widely across plants and businesses, with some part number fields being ten characters long and all numeric, and others being up to thirty characters long and alphanumeric. Some part numbering schemes are random, while other part numbering schemes attempt to embed intelligence about the part or its manufacturing process in the part number. Enterprise-wide operations calendars must be established, in conjunction with the finance organization, since manufacturing plants in a large company often operate on different calendars. Many follow the calendar year rigorously, so a month or quarter might end on any day of the week. Others use a four-four-five–week calendar, so no matter what the calendar month or day, a quarter always ends at the end of the thirteenth week.

Obviously, it's possible to operate a business in this unorganized and confusing manner, but the point is *at what cost* in time and dollars and poor productivity. We want to raise our quest for better business performance to *new* levels—both to the enterprise level and to world-class performance levels. To do this, we need to facilitate clearer communication and understanding across corporate business units, reduce the amount of education and training needed by having more consistent data throughout the corporation, improve software programmer productivity, and have the data defined and managed so that we can more easily search for commonalities across the enterprise.

As McGrath and Hoole note: "Well-connected facilities are useless if employees don't understand each other. Creating a common management 'language'—a universal set of management practices and measurement systems—is also crucial."[2]

The process they describe has to start with fundamental definitions of business terms and data. Then, management practices and sound business processes complete with the right performance measurement systems can be built around the solid data definition foundation.

ESTABLISHING THE CORPORATION'S DATA MANAGEMENT CAPABILITY

The average manufacturing company usually has a kluge of data management systems in place, ranging from ASCII flat files that aren't even database management systems

(DBMS), to old hierarchical design DBMSs like IBM's IMS, to network design DBMSs such as Computer Associate's (formerly Cullinet's) IDMS, to modern relational DBMSs like (but not limited to) IBM's DB2 (for System 370 architecture mainframes) or the one found in IBM's S/38 and AS/400 minicomputers, or those offered by leading software vendors such as Oracle, Sybase, Informix, ASK, and Progress. Each of these requires different methods of access and operation. Each of these vendors is at a different point with regard to data management sophistication and product development needed to accommodate throughout (transactions per second), record updating, backup and recovery, and security. Also, each vendor is at a different place in terms of its ability to handle enterprise-wide distributed data accurately and effectively.

Here is a major opportunity for corporations to standardize on one modern data management approach, and reap some economies of scale with regard to corporate leverage using only one vendor. This will also foster economies of scale in education and training of software personnel, as well as in the speed of future enhancements and implementation and the ability to achieve tighter integration within the company and between the company's application systems (like ELM/MRP/DRP) and its database management and even networking software.

ESTABLISHING THE CORPORATION'S COMPUTING HARDWARE BASE

The computing world has been moving swiftly to distributed microcomputers as the basis for information processing. Mainframes are too costly (inherently, and because they are proprietary), too complex, and carry too much necessary overhead to be anything but large file servers and perhaps telecommunication hubs in the future. Minicomputers are better than mainframes in that they require much less overhead to operate effectively, but they traditionally have had proprietary architectures, a situation that carries serious penalties in today's and tomorrow's open-systems computing environment. It is true that some minis are being "opened up" to run UNIX and Windows NT, although these operating systems are not the definitive basis for an open system. But the fact is that microcomputers, particularly those that are RISC-based, and the ones based on Intel's more traditionally designed Pentium microprocessor, are faster and cheaper than minicomputers. Also, experience in a wide variety of businesses shows that microcomputers in a distributed processing environment can also compete in terms of computing capability against the mainframe and mini-based solutions.

Whether the distributed computing environment, in total, is cheaper is still open to some debate. It is not as convenient to capture all relevant costs when computing is distributed throughout the enterprise, as when it is focused primarily in one information systems department. The "centralists" say that many costs of today's reportedly cheaper distributed open systems computing environment are often overlooked. In addition, the trip down the learning curve to get the enterprise switched over to distributed computing carries with it extensive education and training costs. In the short term, distributed computing may be no more inexpensive than the system it replaces, or it may even be somewhat more expensive. *Even if they are more expensive,* open systems carry many more benefits that make them worthwhile:

- They provide a modularly scalable and flexible computing infrastructure. Change in any direction is easy to accommodate with open systems. Growing and need more workstations? Just add them to the network. Need more computing power for a person or for a special application? Just unplug the old and plug in the new, higher-power workstation. Need more data storage capacity in the network? Just add a bigger file server. Buying new, more sophisticated equipment? Just remove the oldest computers from the bottom of the equipment list and give everyone a "trickle-down" upgrade.

- Applications development or modification goes much faster on microsystems than in the old mainframe environment. Reports and studies show that applications development in the open distributed microcomputer environment goes two to five times faster. This carries with it obvious benefits in programming productivity, but, most important, it gets the applications benefits to the users and the enterprise as a whole more quickly.

- User productivity is higher in the world of the graphical user interface (GUI) that first became popular in the microcomputing world (indeed, first with Apple's Macintosh). The point and click (and often color) environment of the GUI is a more user-friendly and intuitive interface for the average user than the black-and-white character-based screens of the mainframe and mini era. Not only does productivity of the user go up, but eyestrain, fatigue, and errors go down.

THE NEW WORLD OF COMPUTING

It is important to realize that the challenge in today's modern manufacturing corporation is to create the information system infrastructure that empowers each worker with real-time access to the data or information they need to perform their job effectively and satisfy their customers. Corporations must accomplish this in three major areas: engineering systems, business systems, and shop floor systems.

Consider the average information system purchase today. One company spent many months pulling together requirements for a quality reporting system for the shop floor. During this time, they also concentrated on formulating the sales pitch and financial justification to their senior management for this $900,000 system. Because of this company's lack of a modern and comprehensive computing infrastructure, only $200,000 of the $900,000 was allocated for the quality *application* (a fine quality reporting and analysis application package could have been had for one-half that price). The great majority of the money for the project—approximately 75 percent—was to be used to put the computing infrastructure in place on the shop floor. This infrastructure was the same one, by the way, that could have served as the basis for the shop floor material tracking system for the materials management people. Needless to say, the cost justification for this project was difficult under conventional management thinking. In addition, the quality function was having to bear the cost of installing a system that, among others, the materials function should have shared in funding.

In planning for computing in today's and tomorrow's business world, a sensible estimate would be one microcomputer or workstation (either PC or today's UNIX-based workstation) per employee. To some extent, that number depends on how many shop floor workers a business has, for not every shop floor employee needs a computer, even though many computers are needed on the shop floor. But to counter that, people in management, and specifically sales and marketing, are likely to have *three* computers—one in the office, one at home, and one to take in the car or on the airplane! So the real ratio of computers to employees might fall in the range 0.8 to 1:1. Indeed, the 1993 *Computerworld* Premier 100 profile shows over twenty manufacturers already meeting or exceeding this ratio.[3]

That is a far cry from today's environments in many manufacturing companies. In recent informal surveys, the number of people who have real-time access to the data or information they need is usually about 10 percent for engineering data users, and less than 50 percent for business and shop floor data users. So it appears the immediate need in most companies is to get the computing infrastructure established.

Consider what's needed on most shop floors in manufacturing plants today. Not only do the employees need real-time access to scheduling and material movement data, but they also are likely to need access to assembly instructions as lot sizes approach one, as product differentiation and "mass customization" calls for highly customized products built on common platforms, and as the shop floor workforce becomes increasingly filled with people whose primary (or only) language is *not* English. Thus, we can look forward to the benefits of assembly computer workstations that can access geometric data from CAD systems, as well as provide video-based assembly instruction in any of about five languages for each specific product configuration and employee as the product moves through the production line.

Consider how differently we will buy computers and applications once the enterprise-wide computing infrastructure is established. At that point, we will only be doing selective (right down to individual microcomputers or servers) enhancement of the hardware infrastructure. Functionally specialized applications such as quality reporting systems and ELM systems will probably cost well under $100,000, and maybe as little as $5,000 to $10,000! Standard applications such as spreadsheet and word processing software will be priced even below today's $50 to $500. Buying decisions will be made much more quickly by local and lower-level management. Huge projects will not have to be sold and justified up through three or four levels of management, or all the way to the top. Buying new applications or modular enhancements to existing applications will be "no brainer" decisions made quickly and locally (though within enterprise-wide standards). Tomorrow's computing environment will allow a dramatically different way of procuring and maintaining information system elements.

ESTABLISHING THE BASE ELM/MRP/DRP SYSTEMS

As with data definition and database management systems, most manufacturing companies currently have a hodge-podge of manufacturing planning and control systems. In some plants, there is still no "MRP" system at all! Others have MRP-like systems, often patched together with home-grown and poorly documented code over the years. Still others have all, or parts of, first-through-third-generation MRP/DRP software packages installed that represent a variety of software vendors, MRP functional capabilities, computer platforms, operating systems, database management systems, and programming languages.

Ideally, it is good to have one enterprise-wide standard ELM/MRP/DRP system. However, this utopia is not likely to be achieved in practice soon except in a minority of cases. In fact, there may be legitimate cause *today* in large and highly diversified manufacturing companies to have at least two basic ELM application packages—one that is more effective in process manufacturing, and one that is more effective in discrete part manufacturing. No one software package does a leading-edge job of covering both these manufacturing environments.

So the real goal in most manufacturing companies—especially the largest ones—is to *evolve* toward the ideal solution in incremental steps according to the following plan:

1. Catalog and document the diversity of manufacturing planning and control systems in use throughout your corporation, noting the potential differences we have described, especially which modules of the MRP system are installed in each plant. Along with noting installed modules, an attempt should be made to characterize the functionality (or lack of it), especially with regard to master production scheduling, order pegging, allowable time buckets, and basic purchasing functionality (such as purchasing requirements, vendor rating systems, and global vendor sourcing capability). Landvater and Gray's MRP II Standard System description is a good guide for understanding and evaluating base levels of MRP functionality.[4] Also, the diversity of replanning frequencies and time buckets used in each system should be documented.

2. Separate the systems currently in place into three or four categories, such as:

- "Okay for the immediate future."
- "Can be further enhanced and/or implemented."

- "Replace immediately."
- "Must implement an MRP system immediately regardless of vendor and computer hardware/software platform."

Priority should be given to replacing MRP systems from the bottom of this list up, that is, first implementing them where there are none, then replacing the corporation's most dysfunctional and/or obsolete ones. The goal is to quickly make the enterprise operate with some basic level of ELM functionality, which can be enhanced to leading-edge capability in the near future.

3. The ELM organization should work closely with both information system people and operations managers throughout the corporation to standardize the *way the current systems are operated* as much as possible. This involves agreeing on timing cutoffs, standard shop calendars, time bucket size across a minimum standardized planning horizon, frequency of MRP replanning, and the like.

4. Evaluate and select the new ELM system(s) that will form the basis for the corporation's ELM vision over the next five to ten years. Naturally, this selection should be made from vendors who have modern software specifically written for the open distributed systems computing environment and microcomputer-based networks. These vendors should also offer software that works with the leading relational database management systems and most popular network operating systems. These ELM software packages must have the primary ELM functionality built into them in one tightly integrated offering. They should offer the full gamut of order entry/customer service, DRP, master production scheduling, material requirements planning,

capacity requirements planning (infinite and/or finite), and procurement functionality (supplier rating, global sourcing, and supplier history). Naturally, the integrated "financials" that come with such MRP packages today must also be present with leading-edge functionality, too.

It should be noted that there are many excellent MRP packages available today that fill many of these requirements. Most notably missing from some of these packages are (integrated) DRP and the master production schedule logic to drive ELM at a corporate level. Only one or two of them has any real-time replanning capability integrated into the vendor's software today. Moreover, many are lacking the world-class purchasing functionality needed to manage adequately the portion of the business representing 60 percent to 80 percent of product cost in most manufacturing companies.

INTEGRATING JIT CONCEPTS WITH ELM/MRP

Executives in many companies are confused over which "system" to use for materials management and production scheduling—MRP, JIT, or other concepts like OPT or finite scheduling. To shed some light on this question, consider the historical development of each of the three major systems or philosophies above.

- MRP was developed in the United States, originally for use in job shops with their individual shop orders, a material basis, backward scheduling, and infinite capacity planning.
- OPT (optimized production technique) came from Israel through Creative Output, Inc. This philosophy and software package focused on identifying the bottleneck

operation (at a given time) and forward scheduling from it, thus optimizing throughput given that specific bottleneck. It then backward-scheduled all nonbottleneck operations. OPT was never sold as a complete package, as were most MRP packages, but rather was often sold as an adjunct to a full-blown MRP package.

- JIT originated in Japan in response to Taiichi Ohno's observations about how American supermarkets functioned. Implemented first (starting in 1947) at Toyota as the Toyota Production System, it continues to be refined to this day. Its goal is to eliminate waste (*muda*) in *all* forms from all business operations. It is more than an inventory reduction tool because inventory is only one form of waste. JIT demands a relatively smooth schedule, and therefore functions best in a repetitive manufacturing environment buffered by large finished goods stocks. JIT may or may not be computerized.

Each of these systems or philosophies is capable of delivering powerful benefits to manufacturers that implement them effectively. The main thing to recognize about these three systems is that they are not mutually exclusive. While developed from three different perspectives, manufacturing planning and control systems of the future such as ELM will incorporate the best of all three philosophies. The point is not which system to use, but how to effectively blend the best features of MRP and JIT and OPT into a flexible, real-time, and user-friendly ELM system for planning and scheduling production and logistics within an enterprise.

Whether or not a company ever utilizes the forward finite scheduling found in OPT and some other software packages, it is virtually certain that it will have to use some combination of MRP and JIT to be capable of world-class scheduling and materials management. Imagine a continuous spectrum from the simplest factory at one end, capable of being operated effectively with a purely manual JIT system, visible indicators, and the like, to a highly complex CIM-based lights-out "factory of the future" at the other end. The key challenge for most manufacturers, given the nature of their products and processes, production volumes, and supplier/distribution channels, is to determine where on that spectrum they should be as a function of time and then develop a phased plan to get the entire enterprise there as quickly as possible. This plan should also move the enterprise toward progressively increasing sophistication and performance levels in the future.

PROGRESSING TOWARD ELM

As we noted earlier, the ELM vision must first be established for the enterprise. Then, the ELM implementation schedule concentrates on moving from two directions toward the ELM vision. In the top-down direction, the goal is to put in place the organization and enterprise-wide software—for telecommunications and particularly for order entry, DRP (if needed), and corporate, group, or division-level master production scheduling. Working up from the bottom, all plants must be upgraded to some common level of MRP/JIT systems capability and operating standardization.

There may be highly complex production environments in the company where all the features of a full MRP package are needed, including infinite capacity planning, if not finite capacity planning or scheduling. These systems are likely to be needed in plants building heavy machinery where parts counts are high, engineering changes are frequent, lead times are long due to complex machining, fabrication and assembly requirements, many product options or configurations complicate the production environment, and there is a large supplier base. It is in these shop floor environments, of course, that feedback to the MRP-generated plan in the form of bar-coded (generally) material tracking systems is so important. Management must attempt to utilize all the principles and concepts of JIT possible in such plants, such as quick setups, minimum lot sizes, and minimum waste in moving and inspecting parts. But the size and complexity of such products and manufacturing processes preclude running anything less than a full-blown MRP application.

In less complex production environments, with fewer and simpler products and processes, it is possible to use the *planning* capabilities of MRP and the *execution* capabilities of JIT in a highly effective combination. For production scheduling purposes at a high level, MRP can be used both to generate a master production schedule and to summarize time-phased material requirements for suppliers. The master production schedule would generate production line rates or absolute requirements in units for each product platform (and configuration of it) for any time period.

But, in this case, the execution of the master production schedule would be by a JIT "pull" system, based on master production schedule demand. In other words, individual part production schedules would not be developed in the MRP system for parts and subassemblies under the master production schedule level. Instead, kanban signs, used in conjunction with standard material handling containers, would trigger all part production or parts supply in the manufacturing and assembly of each product. Material tracking would be simplified, and bar-coded scanning might just be limited to the point at which the final product emerges from the final assembly work cell, where each final product would be scanned and the parts it contained would be relieved from the raw material/parts inventory by back-flushing.

There may be, in the simplest of production environments, no need for *any* computerized production planning or scheduling, or materials management. In such plants, typically one product with a very simple production process, master production schedule requirements could simply be dumped into a spreadsheet or posted manually on a board using numbers or colored tags or the like. Even in these simple environments, though, the final product will still need to be "entered" into the world of electronic inventory and distribution management, probably through a bar-code scanner.

Note that in all the cases mentioned, one of management's goals is to simplify the production environment as much as possible, using good business process reengineering principles, and the elements of JIT, TQM, sound product and process design, and modern information systems we have referred to earlier in this book. But only so much of this is possible or practical. Enterprises will need a variety of standard, yet more sophisticated, approaches to managing materials and production scheduling within each major type of plant environment.

CHAPTER 8

Enterprise Logistics Management in Tomorrow's Business Environment

THE REALITY OF ELM

There is no question that the vision and the reality of ELM is becoming more apparent in business around the globe today. Xerox Corporation, with about $15 billion in document processor revenue in 1992, certainly represents the leading edge of ELM thinking in the United States, if not the world. In 1989, after substantial implementation of a world-class manufacturing program, Xerox embarked on a new global program named "CLAM"—Central Logistics and Asset Management. The central elements of the program:

- Created a corporate logistics group to drive logistics planning and execute lead time reduction globally;
- Converted to a pull system throughout Xerox's supply chain;

- Implemented joint service agreements between manufacturing and operating companies;
- Changed performance measures to business process basis, emphasizing lead time and cost reduction;
- Formed benchmarking partnerships to understand best logistics practices and processes; and
- Developed global pilot programs to evaluate process changes.

The results Xerox obtained from just the first thirty-six months of CLAM included:

- Total supply chain lead time reductions of 50 percent confirmed by pilots;
- Reduced total inventory by $650 million (33 percent);
- Asset recovery and supply chain cost reduced by $150 million (15 percent);
- Total inventory as a percent of sales reduced from 19 percent to 14 percent (26 percent); and
- Customer satisfaction measures up two to nine percentage points against new, tougher metrics.[1]

All these results were accomplished with a partial (corporate) implementation and *before* Xerox acquired a real-time replanning capability for use with their legacy MRP system, which has since cut another week from their materials planning cycle! Utilizing the results of a "P3" (production planning process) project and CLAM, Xerox was able to reduce the days of stock of one major product from seventy in 1990 to thirty-four in 1993 with no reduction in customer service.[2]

Note that with the savings Xerox has achieved, the issue of cost justification for the implementation of ELM is trivial to nonexistent. Savings on inventory carrying cost *alone*, figured at 20 percent carrying cost per year, is $130 million per year (forever, unless the inventory goes up again). (Total inventory carrying cost more likely should be 30 percent to 40 percent per year.) Even at a mere 10 percent carrying cost rate, savings are $65 million per year—a figure that greatly exceeds any cost for systems development or acquisition and integration, user education and training, and ELM implementation.

THE INEVITABILITY OF ELM

The inevitability of ELM is part of a larger realization about the value of information in business. Business is becoming more information-intensive. Stephan H. Haeckel captures this trend when he points out:

If there is such a thing as sustainable advantage, it is based on consistently superior information and knowledge. . . . Reducing uncertainty is [information's] defined function.[3]

Later, he comments:

Information as *action-agent,* rather than symbolic record of the results of action, is the concept behind recently emerging business strategies aimed at enhancing organization responsiveness to market change. Getting information off the bench and onto the playing field transforms it from an expense of doing business to an asset *for* doing business [italics mine].[4]

This directly reflects the experience of United Parcel Service (UPS), which about six years ago was forced to address the fact that they were losing business despite their cadre of 3,000 industrial engineers who ensured that UPS was the low-*cost* package handler and forwarder in the business. But, in reinforcement of the triumph of time-based competition over cost-based competition, Federal Express had been able to move faster and satisfy their customers more completely (despite not being the low-price provider) because they had the *information* the customer wanted as to where their package was, had it been delivered, and who signed for it. UPS, realizing they had no choice, invested more than $2 billion over the past six years to have the industry's most advanced information system. Not only have they seen a surge in business and profits, but even more interesting is that Federal Express is now being forced to upgrade their information system to keep up. UPS's chairman, Kent "Oz" Nelson, said, "We realized that the leader in information management will be the leader in international package distribution—period."[5]

As we have noted all along, the goal is to turn the *art* of running a manufacturing business into the *science* of more effectively running such a business for the satisfaction of its customers. One of the main ways we can accomplish this is to reduce the uncertainty surrounding the actions of the enterprise's customers, manufacturing plants, and suppliers. Hewlett-Packard has done a great deal of fine work on this task. In a recent *Sloan Management Review* article on supply management, Tom Davis of H-P shows that the root causes of H-P's inventory break out roughly as shown on page 127.[6]

It's important to understand that this is what H-P finds after a decade of pursuing world-class manufacturing performance, with vigorous attention to TQM, supplier excellence, and integrated MRP/JIT. Other less ambitious, able, and knowledgeable manufacturers would show much higher percentages of manufacturing process, supply, and

Percent of Total Inventory	Root causes
~35% to 45%	Minimum stock (WIP, pipeline, review periods)
~5%	Manufacturing process variance
~5%	Supply variance
~45% to 55%	Demand variance

minimum stock, and, of course, much higher overall inventory levels.[7]

THE REVOLUTION IN RETAILING

Tied to both of the above points is the tremendous revolution in retailing that is happening today. This has been accomplished in two ways, as Peter Drucker eloquently points out:

Wal-Mart's success, for example, rests in large measure on its redefining retailing as the *moving* of merchandise, rather than its sale. This led to the integration of the entire process—all the way from the manufacturer's machine to the selling floor—on the basis of "real-time" information about customer purchases.

In the same article, he points out that the definition of retail service has been changed by retailing leaders.

For traditional merchants, service means salespeople who personally take care of an individual customer. But the new retailers employ very few salespeople. Service to them means that customers *do not need a salesperson* [italics mine], do not have to spend time trying to find one, do not have to ask, do not have to wait. It means that the customers know where goods are the moment they enter the store, in what colors and sizes, and at what price. It means providing *information*.[8]

So what does this portend for retailing? It will start with the consumer no longer having to go to a store for most items. Most shopping will be performed by utilizing a combination of interactive television, telephone, computer, and virtual reality. Already, QVC Network, Inc., and Home Shopping Network, Inc.'s television shopping services continue to capture market share from more traditional forms of retailing. Customers will even transact more of their billing or checkout work traditionally executed by others. At many gas stations today, customers use their credit cards and pump-mounted scanners to perform their own checkout activity without any help from the retailer. The checkout is also accomplished more quickly.

Wal-Mart is well known for having world-class information systems. As *Forbes* business magazine noted recently in a major article on the revolution in distribution:

> Wal-Mart stores have only about 10% of their square footage for inventory compared with the average store, which has 25% of its space not used for selling. . . . With new information systems and distribution programs that Kmart has developed . . . the company has been able to reduce the inventory carried in its distribution centers by 20%, while increasing sales by 15%.[9]

One of the globe's finest retailers is 7-Eleven Japan. With about 5,000 7-Eleven stores in Japan averaging only 1,080 square feet apiece, 7-Eleven Japan uses information systems extensively to track its store items (some 40 percent of these items are perishable and have to be replenished daily) and follow the whims of its customers, including knowing which products sell better at different times of the same day. Richard Rawlinson, managing director of Monitor Company's (a U.S.-based consulting organization) Tokyo office comments on 7-Eleven Japan: "No other retailer in the world has defined its business so tightly around information."[10]

Does their intensive use of information technology pay off for them? Well, 7-Eleven Japan is able to command a royalty fee for its franchises of ~43 percent of annual gross profits, versus its closest competitor's 35 percent. In addition, its knowledge from its information systems (and its sales volume) "give [it] enormous leverage over suppliers, helping its franchisees get better prices and preferred access to hit items."[11]

Does 7-Eleven Japan's extensive use of information technology pay off for its franchisees? Well, their average daily store sales are more than 30 percent above their closest competitor. In addition, their superior distribution because of their better information systems means that they have been able to cut the number of truck deliveries from thirty-four a day in 1980 to just twelve currently. Thus, store clerks can spend more time in the store helping customers, not handling deliveries, and fewer clerks are likely to be needed.

Does 7-Eleven Japan's extensive use of information systems pay off for its customers? Yes. They get lower prices, a better selection, *and* the ability to purchase new services, such as the ability to pay insurance and utility bills at the store.

An especially interesting comment about 7-Eleven's use of information systems relative to the points in this chapter comes from Kaz Uchida, a vice president at the Boston Consulting Group's Tokyo office: "7-Eleven's [information] system *is a learning device. As the process is repeated, ordering precision increases.*"[12]

It is sad to note that the U.S. Southland-owned 7-Eleven stores (Southland is 64 percent owned by 7-Eleven Japan and Ito-Yokado) are nowhere near the advanced ELM concepts of 7-Eleven Japan's stores and logistics organization.

New software tools like Trilogy Development Corporation's Sales-Builder are emerging that will make it easier for customers to configure their own product from a manufacturer's electronic catalog, and get confirmation that their product as specified is buildable and what it will cost for that unique combination of product and services. Not only will this software make it easier and faster for the customer to order in an error-free manner, but it also will shift work away from the providers, thus lowering their cost, resulting in fewer errors in incoming orders, again saving the manufacturer and customer from expensive or time-consuming mistakes.

Retail goods will flow through the value-added pipeline as a result of consumer pull, rather than manufacturer push. Procter & Gamble, a $30 billion U.S. consumer goods company, for instance, has been a leader in this move away from giant promotional push programs that wreaked havoc on its distribution, manufacturing, and supplier network, as well as its customers. Because of the JIT emphasis on the flow of materials and goods throughout the entire value-added pipeline, the size of an average transaction will decrease, while the frequency of transactions increases. Howard Anderson, managing director of the Yankee Group, points out that "everything is on consignment—what those retailers are doing is basically renting shelf space to their suppliers. So, the metric becomes: gross profit per cubic foot per hour."[13]

Note the implications on cash flow and finance as everything moves to a consignment basis. Instead of getting paid when the buying organization buys the product, the supplier won't get paid until the buying organization *sells* the product. One example of this today is that General Motor's Saturn plant pays its suppliers when their products come off the line assembled in the finished car, not when they receive them.

A NEW WAY OF LOOKING AT MANUFACTURING

This leads to an interesting new way of looking at manufacturing, as Esther Dyson pointed out recently. She likens the operation of a manufacturing plant to the operation of an airline, where yield management is the name of the game in maximizing revenue. In doing so, airlines carefully manage an entire range of different prices possible for each seat sold, depending on the customer, the route, when the ticket is bought, and what time of the day, week, month, or year it is. She suggests to manufacturers:

> Suppose you start to think of selling goods as selling time on your manufacturing line—embodied as products. Suddenly, your manufacturing line is something to be scheduled as tightly as an airline.... *But most manufacturers aren't acting from good information* [italics mine]. They just know that they have a four-week lead time and they quote that regularly. They don't know how to price a two-week order or whether they could make money delivering next Friday but not next Wednesday. They don't manage for underutilized capacity or overbooking the way the airlines do.... But that is about to change.[14]

Consider a $500 million manufacturer working two eight-hour shifts for fifty-two weeks a year. What's the value in revenue potential of its production time?—$120,192 per hour, $2,003 per minute, and $33 per *second!* How do we make sure no revenue is lost to downtime? How can we maximize the yield of revenue from production?

Just as we think we're beginning to get our arms around managing enterprise logistics, a whole new competitive paradigm such as this concept comes along to freshly challenge manufacturers. The winners will be those with the vision, the knowledge, and the real-time information to manage their businesses more effectively.

As we saw with 7-Eleven Japan, some of the Japanese have not been slow to realize what's going on in the world of manufacturing and advanced information systems. As an example of their thinking, Professor Jinichiro Nakane, of the System Science Institute of Waseda University in Tokyo, comments, "This *post-JIT* environment places an emphasis on information systems—not only those that communicate customer design orders, but also on electronic production-control systems [italics mine]."[15]

Indicative of Japan's Sony Corporation's thinking, one of their executives commented, "Sony is committed to the Computer Integrated Enterprise. . . . The goal is to speed up our business. . . . That's strategic."[16]

Consider Kao Corporation, Japan's largest soap and cosmetic company, the sixth largest such company in the world, about $5 billion in size. They have one integrated information system from R&D through shipping. Kao delivers goods within twenty-four hours to 280,000 shops in Japan, with an average order size of seven items. Their information systems are linked to several hundred point-of-sale terminals in stores, as well as to salespersons' handheld computers. So sophisticated are their information systems that their accountants can close their books at the end of the year by noon of the first day of the new year! Kao's average inventory as a percent of sales is about 8 to 9 percent, about one-half of Wal-Mart's and Kmart's.[17]

Don't sell the Japanese short on their understanding of the benefits of information technology and their skill in implementing ELM.

THE DRIVING FORCES BEHIND THE MOVE TO ELM

So ELM will fast become an inexorable reality, driven by three primary factors. The first of these is the *intensity of global competition and global customers' continuing demand for lower cost and better service.* For example, we used to consider the cost of a 100 percent service level to be prohibitive under classical inventory management theory. Yet, suppliers to America's mass market stores like Kmart are being told that 100 percent service level is critical to keep Kmart's business. This is having a drastic impact on suppliers' plans to implement new kinds of thinking and performance in manufacturing, distribution, and information systems.

Second, *no executive interested in his or her company's survival, growth, and prosperity (not to mention his or her own tenure in office) can afford to ignore the enormous benefits that have already accrued to the early implementers of (in most cases) just part of the ELM vision.* We have seen many examples of these benefits in this book. Probably Xerox and Wal-Mart represent the U.S. companies that are farthest along toward the ELM vision. Many other fine companies worldwide are working toward a solution, but usually from the bottom up, without sufficient *corporate* understanding and emphasis.

Third, of course, is the *continuing tremendous rate of change in information technology and of our understanding of how to effectively put that technology to work for the benefit of manufacturers.* In a recent *Harvard Business Review* article, Stephan Haeckel and Richard Nolan discuss the notion of an intelligent company that can excel in dealing with the complexity of today's and tomorrow's business world. First, they establish a complexity index to measure the universe each business competitor deals with. Information-based, these factors include the number of information sources a business has, the number of business elements to be coordinated, and the number and types of relationships between these elements.

To these factors, in the most general case, let's add a fourth factor: *the number and types of data a business has to deal with.* Manufacturers have three types of data to manage effectively: business (alphanumeric) data, found in accounting, sales and marketing, and MRP systems; engineering (geometric) data that describes products, found in computer aided design systems; and real-time (literally) process automation and control data, found in control systems that might run a paper-making line or a sheet steel rolling mill. Thus, manufacturers, with all three types of data to manage, face a far more complex world than a bank, where only alphanumeric data have to be managed.

Haeckel and Nolan then go on to describe the notion of "corporate I.Q.," which they describe as: "[the] institutional ability to deal with complexity, that is, [the] ability to capture, share, and extract meaning from marketplace signals."[18]

Again, this definition of corporate IQ could be strengthened by amending it to include marketplace, company-wide, and business partner signals, for the two new sources are often as important as those signals received from the marketplace. Haeckel and Nolan describe three factors that influence corporate IQ: connecting, or the ability to access knowledge and information ("connecting" goes to the

essence of information system coverage and real-timeness);
sharing, or the ability to integrate and share information;
and structuring, or the ability to extract meaning (information) from data. Note that all of these factors are precisely
the themes that ELM directly addresses. Connecting, sharing, and structuring logistics information is the lifeblood of
a manufacturer's successful existence. A manufacturing
company's ability to excel in this area is a fundamental key
to competitive advantage today, and even more certainly in
the future.

Information and management are becoming more real-
time. Business data are becoming more plentiful and
more accurate thanks to better definition and the use of
automated (and largely error-free) scanners. Systems are
becoming more seamless or integrated. All this makes possible the elevation of logistics management to a higher
enterprise level. Our ability to manage more effectively has
taken us from the individual worker level to a departmental
level to a plant level to a business process level, and now is
taking us to the enterprise level. Beyond the enterprise level
lies the emerging reality of the virtual or extended enterprise where transient business entities are formed from
segments of more than one corporation to address one
aspect of a market need that may only exist for a short
period of time. This ability to manage higher and higher
levels of complexity cost-effectively is largely due to modern information technology.

A FUTURE MANUFACTURER'S ELM SCENARIO

It's the year 2001. Ever Able Manufacturing (EAM) produces consumer products. Orders come to them 100
percent electronically from a wide variety of customers—

individuals from their home or office, distributors (the few that are left), and mass market chains. EAM operates twenty-four hours a day, seven days a week, fifty-two weeks a year through a network of small plants and design centers around the world.

Global customer orders, carefully screened for proper configuration and costing/pricing by advanced expert systems-based software, flow real-time into the corporation's master production schedule, part of its enterprise logistics management system. Orders routinely are flowed to the company's global plants depending on a real-time analysis of product/process capability, available capacity, available tooling, materials availability, labor/skill availability, currency conditions, political risk, shipping cost, and proximity to the customer or supplier. Other criteria that may determine plant assignment are whether least time or least cost is of overriding concern, and yield management criteria about what each individual customer is willing to pay and/or wait to get their product in whatever time frame they want it.

Each plant's material requirements are flowed on a real-time basis to their suppliers, automatically selected, of course, by supplier rating systems that have statistical data on performance factors such as cost, quality, lead time, delivery reliability, and degree of product and process design expertise. Each requirement is sent electronically to a supplier, where, after it passes through their MRP system, an electronic commitment is automatically sent back to EAM promising that the supplier can and will make the desired part and have it available at the right time for EAM. Planning for EAM's entire supply chain, averaging four levels, the pass down the hierarchy and the commit and/or modification back up the hierarchy to EAM—generally takes no more than thirty minutes, and only requires the intervention of one or more planners about 25 percent of the time.

Products are produced and shipped within two days of order, usually within eighteen hours. At any time, any customer can log in to EAM's ELM database and ascertain where their product is and that there have been no quality problems with its manufacture. This also applies to the product in transit. Thanks to global satellite positioning technology, everyone knows where any product in transit is within a range of one-quarter mile.

EAM's entire ELM system exists, as do most other companies, in a state of "dynamic tension," where changes ripple through the entire value-added pipeline in a continuous manner. Large perturbations such as huge order drop-ins or cancellations outside of the parameters controlled by each company in the supply chain are filtered out of the real-time on-line operations system into off-line real-time simulation systems that planners at every level can use to examine the effects of such large-scale potential disturbances. Once it is determined how these will be handled, they are let into the real-time system.

Goods flow through the entire value-added pipeline on consignment, paid for only when they are used by all but the final end user or customer, who pays upon receipt.

At any time and from any location, employees (with appropriate need to know and security checks) can access the global real-time ELM system in any level of detail from corporate or business group summary information to a particular customer's order, or right into a shop floor cell manufacturing a particular item. There is one set of accurate data that drives the company from receipt of the customer order, and one set of financial books and measures upon which performance reporting is based. There are no surprises, anywhere. Out-of-normal conditions are immediately identified so that multifunctional employee teams from around the globe can get to work fixing them at once.

ACHIEVING THE BENEFITS OF ELM

After becoming aware of and buying into the vision and benefits of ELM, the key question most executives ask is "How do we get started with its implementation?" Here are nine steps to doing so.

1. *Establish a corporate-level ELM vision.* This step is critical because it both paints a state of "betterness" and serves to inspire people with its potential for them and their company. It also plants a bit of "FUD"—fear, uncertainty, and doubt—that if the company doesn't aggressively get on with implementing their vision in their company, their competitors might well beat them to it.

2. *Create the corporate ELM business performance improvement plan.* Here, the strategic plan and accompanying program to translate that plan into operating reality are created with goals for significant improvement in the corporation's logistics business processes.

3. *Develop senior management understanding, support, and commitment.* Without senior management buy-in and aggressive support, a program of this scope, complexity, and organizational impact will go nowhere, or nowhere *sufficiently fast.* Benchmarking, education and training, and continual selling of the ELM vision are necessary to obtain and *maintain* this executive-level support.

4. *Establish the foundation information management systems and telecommunication infrastructure.* Information—real-time, integrated, quickly accessible by anyone, anywhere, who needs to know—is the key to competitive advantage in ELM and business in general. Don't let the lack of superb information systems be the bottleneck throttling world-class enterprise-wide logistics management.

5. *Implement the ability to perform real-time ELM/DRP/MRP planning and analysis.* Reengineer your corporation's planning process. Given the increasing complexity and volatility of today's global business environment, the ability to plan, analyze, and understand the implications from such analysis is a key to effective management. Once any one of your competitors has this capability and you don't, you're in trouble. Make sure you're the first, not the last, to obtain and use it.

6. *Achieve business process excellence in the customer order to delivery and materials management/operations scheduling business processes.* World-class information systems cannot make up for faulty or wasteful business practices. Perform the reengineering on these critical business processes first.

7. *Educate and train your corporation's employees about the successful implementation and operation of ELM.* Education and training are keys to building core competencies in any company. In the end, people will be the ultimate differentiators in your company's quest for competitive advantage. How you build, capture, and access your company's intellectual capital is critical to enduring world-class business performance.

8. *Implement new enterprise-wide customer-focused world-class performance measures.* The selection and standardized use of these new performance measures should "pull" (in a JIT sense) company business units and corporate performance toward world-class standards. They must be customer-focused. They must encourage the right new actions, not reinforce yesterday's success (or mediocrity) paradigms.

9. *Persevere toward successfully implementing ELM.* The scope and rate of change in pursuit of ELM will be enormous. Distracting fads and "fires" will appear. People will change their jobs and come and go. Business and profits will go through their ups and downs. But those who work incrementally and steadfastly toward the vision with constancy of purpose will be the winners in tomorrow's global business community. Make sure your company is one of them. Get started now.

Notes

Introduction

1. Pittiglio, Rabin, Todd & McGrath presentation at Carp Systems International's User Conference, June, 1993.

2. Peter F. Drucker, "The Economy's Power Shift," *Wall Street Journal*, September 24, 1992, op. ed. page.

Chapter 3: Reengineering the Five Basic Business Processes

1. Thomas H. Davenport, *Process Innovation* (Boston: Harvard Business School Press, 1993).

2. "H-P's IT Solutions Optimize Critical Business Processes," *Manufacturing Automation* (November 1992): 1.

3. Esther Dyson, "Airlines Could Teach Manufacturers a Thing or Two," *Computerworld* (May 17, 1993): 29.

4. At least three good sources on business process reengineering are:

Thomas G. Gunn, *21st Century Manufacturing: Creating Winning Business Performance* (New York: Harper Business, 1992), chap. 3.

Thomas H. Davenport, *Process Innovation* (Boston: Harvard Business School Press, 1993).

Michael Hammer and James Champy, *Reengineering the Corporation* (New York: Harper Business, 1993).

5. Ray Stata, "Letters to the Editor," *Harvard Business Review* (September–October 1993): 190.

Chapter 4: Understanding Today's Manufacturing Planning and Control Systems

1. Thomas G. Gunn, *21st Century Manufacturing: Creating Winning Business Performance* (New York: Harper Business, 1992), 279–85.

2. Ibid., exhibit 8.2, 160.

3. Eliyahu Goldratt and Jeff Cox, *The Goal: Excellence In Manufacturing* (Croton-on-Hudson, NY: North River Press, Inc., 1984).

4. Yasuhiro Monden, *Toyota Production System* (Norcross, GA: Industrial Engineering and Management Press, Institute of Industrial Engineers, 1983).

5. Alex Taylor III, "How Toyota Copes with Hard Times," *Fortune* (January 25, 1993): 78–81.

6. Joseph Orlicky, *Material Requirements Planning* (New York: McGraw-Hill Book Company, 1975), 28.

7. Robert W. Hall, *Driving the Productivity Machine* (American Production and Inventory Control Society, 1981), chap. 5.

Chapter 5: Real-Time Operations

1. Author's notes from meeting on June 29, 1993.

Chapter 6: What's Needed to Implement ELM: The Management Factors

1. Michael E. McGrath and Richard W. Hoole, "Manufacturing's New Economies of Scale," *Harvard Business Review* (May–June 1992): 94–102.

2. Benson P. Shapiro et al., "Staple Yourself to an Order," *Harvard Business Review* (July–August 1992): 113–22.

3. "Organizational Learning—The Key to Management Innovation," *Sloan Management Review* (Spring 1989): 63–64.

4. McGrath and Hoole, "Manufacturing's New Economies of Scale," 94–102.

5. Ibid.

6. Bob Malchione, "Make Performance Gages Perform," *Industry Week* (June 17, 1991): 67.

Chapter 7: What's Needed to Implement ELM: The Technical Factors

1. Wayne Eckerson, "TI's Global Net Is Instrument of Success," *Network World* (November 25, 1991): 34–37, 48.

2. Michael E. McGrath and Richard W. Hoole, "Manufacturing's New Economies of Scale," *Harvard Business Review* (May–June 1992): 94–102.

3. Premier 100 issue, *Computerworld*, September 13, 1993.

4. Darryl V. Landvater and Christopher D. Gray, *MRPII Standard System* (Essex Junction, VT: Oliver Wight Limited Publications, Inc., 1989).

Chapter 8: ELM in Tomorrow's Business Environment

1. Pittiglio, Rabin, Todd & McGrath presentation at Carp Systems International's User Conference, June 1993.

2. Xerox Corporation presentation at Carp Systems International's User Conference, June 1993.

3. Stephan H. Haeckel, *Managing the Information-Intensive Firm of 2001*, IBM Advanced Business Institute Paper # M2001, February 1992.

4. Ibid.

5. Peter Coy, "The New Realism in Office Systems," *Business Week* (June 15, 1992): 128–33.

6. Tom Davis, "Effective Supply Chain Management," *Sloan Management Review* (Summer 1993): 35–46.

7. For another superb article on supply chain management, see:

Hau L. Lee and Corey Billington, "Managing Supply Chain Inventory: Pitfalls and Opportunities," *Sloan Management Review* (Spring 1992): 65–73.

8. Peter F. Drucker, "The Retail Revolution," *Wall Street Journal*, July 15, 1993, op. ed. page.

9. Gale Eisenstodt, "Information Power," *Forbes* (June 21, 1993): 44–45.

10. Ibid.

11. Ibid.

12. Ibid.

13. "The New Impact of EDI," *Information Week*, Special Advertising Report (March 15, 1993): 1A–11A.

14. Esther Dyson, "Airlines Could Teach Manufacturers a Thing or Two," *Computerworld* (May 17, 1993): 29.

15. John Teresko, Factory Automation Special Report, *Industry Week* (September 2, 1991): 50.

16. Clinton Wilder, "The Japan View," *Computerworld* (August 13, 1990): 10–12.

17. Thomas A. Stewart, "Brace for Japan's Hot New Strategy," *Fortune* (September 21, 1992): 62–74.

18. Stephan H. Haeckel and Richard L. Nolan, "Managing by Wire," *Harvard Business Review* (September–October 1993): 122–32.

Glossary

ACTIVITY-BASED COSTING (ABC). A form of cost management in which overhead is assigned to products based only on the activities associated with each unique product. As opposed to traditional cost accounting, in which overhead is allocated to all products uniformly based usually on some volume-related activity such as labor or machine hours.

ALLOCATION. A method of assigning and reserving inventory for a specific customer order.

ALPHANUMERIC. Data made up of either numbers or letters or both.

APPLICATION SYSTEM. Computer software written to perform business functions and solve business problems, as opposed to operating system or database management software.

ARTIFICIAL INTELLIGENCE (AI). An early term for expert systems.

AUTOMOTIVE INDUSTRIES ACTION GROUP (AIAG). An automotive industry trade association.

AVAILABLE TO PROMISE (ATP). The available or uncommitted portion of a manufacturer's inventory or planned production. The difference between production and sales in any given time period.

BACKFLUSHING. A technique for relieving inventory, performed *after* manufacturing a part of a product or subassembly by multiplying the number of completed units times the unit's bill of materials and relieving that quantity of parts from inventory.

BACKLOG. All customer orders that remain to be manufactured and delivered to the customer.

BACKWARD SCHEDULING. Scheduling backward from the order due date by the time each operation takes, in order to arrive at an order start date.

BANDWIDTH. The signal-carrying capacity of a telecommunications medium, analogous to the diameter of a water pipe.

BATCH (COMPUTER OPERATION). A group of jobs to be run on a computer at one time with the same program.

BENCHMARKING. The comparison of a company's business practices and performance measures with those of other companies, particularly with those practices and measures of world-class companies or business processes.

BILL OF MATERIALS (BOM). A listing of all parts that make up a product. This listing can show all materials, parts, tools, or subassemblies and be created in various degrees of accuracy for either rough-cut or detailed planning.

BILL OF OPERATIONS. A bill that combines the materials (with product structure information) and the routing so that the complete sequence of events and materials needed to make a product is shown.

BUCKETLESS. A feature of an MRP system in which all time-phased data are internally accounted for in not more than daily time buckets, regardless of whether it later is grouped and reported in larger time segments. In the future, the minimal time bucket for a bucketless system may well be hours or minutes.

BUSINESS PROCESS. The complete set of activities necessary to execute a major element of business, such as customer order to delivery.

BUSINESS PROCESS REENGINEERING (BPR). The improvement of business processes by a cross-functional team that first seeks to understand and document the entire process, then simplifies and removes the waste from it, then applies information systems to improve the speed and quality of the process as well as improve its flexibility and the productivity of the people associated with it.

CAPACITY REQUIREMENTS PLANNING (CRP). The planning of future capacity needs by projecting machine or labor loads in a time-phased manner. See infinite and finite capacity planning.

CLIENT SERVER (COMPUTER ARCHITECTURE). A form of networked distributed computing in which the user operates a client computer (workstation or PC) and, in doing so, usually asks for data or applications from a server located somewhere else in the computing environment. The client is responsible for the user interface. Applications and network operating duties can be shared in several different forms between the client and server. It is not uncommon for the user's everyday applications (e.g., spreadsheet or word processing) to reside on the client machine. A server is typically a special computer dedicated to printing or data management.

COMPUTER AIDED DESIGN (CAD). The use of a computer to capture the design geometry of a part or product. This design is then stored electronically in an engineering database.

COMPUTER AIDED ENGINEERING (CAE). The use of a variety of computer-based analytical software to analyze a part's design, for example, finite element modeling analysis to analyze for mechanical stress and strain.

COMPUTER INTEGRATED MANUFACTURING (CIM). The integration of all information (engineering, business, and process control) involved in the total spectrum of manufacturing activity.

CONSIGNMENT. Material or products in the hands of the next business entity or person in the distribution chain that remain the property of the supplier or manufacturer until their sale or use.

CPK RATIO. The product specification range divided by the process capability range, adjusted to center the process on the target value.

CUM SCHEDULING. Scheduling by cumulative number of units produced. For instance, in week 43, units 15,560 through

16,420 will be scheduled and produced. The schedule would show it in exactly this way.

DATABASE MANAGEMENT SYSTEM (DBMS). The software that manages data in an information system. It usually includes a data dictionary or repository used to define the data and the relationship of each data element to another.

DATA DICTIONARY. A repository of the definition of terms by which a company does business. It would specify, for instance, that part numbers will follow the convention of XX–XXXX, where each X is a numerical character from 0 to 9.

DEMAND PULL. Wherein a customer order immediately triggers a commensurate demand or factory order for only the customer's specific product and quantity ordered.

DEPENDENT DEMAND. Demand directly related to or derived from the demand of other items, as with those parts linked by bills of materials.

DISCRETE PRODUCT. A product made up of distinct parts or components, as opposed to a liquid or gas.

DISTRIBUTED SYSTEMS. Refers to the distribution of computing power, computing function, or data and data management in a multinode computer architecture.

DISTRIBUTION RESOURCE PLANNING (DRP). A software package that is used to determine inventory replenishment needs at branch warehouses in a distribution network, and to aggregate those needs in a time-phased manner back to their supplying sources as input to their master production schedules. The resource planned can also be, at a minimum, warehouse space, shipping mode (truck or rail or airplane space), or manpower.

ECONOMIC ORDER QUANTITY (EOQ). A method of calculating order quantity (lot size) that relates ordering cost to holding cost given the assumption of constant demand for the product. Specifically, the economic order quantity equals the square root of [(two times the annual demand times the ordering cost) divided by the annual holding cost].

ELECTRONIC DATA INTERCHANGE (EDI). The direct transfer of information between computers according to standardized information formats and communication protocols.

ENTERPRISE LOGISTICS MANAGEMENT (ELM). The science of managing the total logistics environment from global suppliers through the company's manufacturing plants through distribution to the final end user in a manufacturing company. This includes the two logistics subbusiness processes of customer order to delivery and materials management, as well as operations scheduling.

EXPERT SYSTEM. A computing system consisting of a knowledge base and an inference engine that codifies a set of rules developed by experienced people to arrive at answers to a problem.

EXPLOSION (BILL OF MATERIAL). A process in which a bill of materials (or recipe) is multiplied by the number of units to be made, and the gross requirements for each part number are aggregated.

FILE SERVER. A computer that serves as a data storage and management device in a network.

FINITE CAPACITY PLANNING. Loading a factory or work center only to its capacity. This process automatically schedules lower-priority items into the next available time period if the current time period's capacity is fully utilized.

FLEXIBLE MANUFACTURING SYSTEMS (FMS). A group of more than two computer-based machine tools combined with integrated material handling and quality control equipment to produce a family of parts with similar product or process attributes. Two machines or less would constitute a flexible manufacturing cell.

FORWARD SCHEDULING. Scheduling a process from a start date forward by operation time to arrive at a finish or ship date.

FOURTH GENERATION (COMPUTER SOFTWARE). A higher-level software programming language than typical third-generation languages such as COBOL or FORTRAN. 4GLs often are natural language, and considerably easier to use than earlier-generation computer languages.

GRAPHICAL USER INTERFACE (GUI). A user interface displayed on a computer CRT screen that is rich in its use of graphics and point-and-click methods that use icons, pull-down menus, and pop-up windows. The Apple Macintosh was the first commercial example of a GUI-based computer. Other examples today are Microsoft's Windows 3.1, X Windows, Motif, and Open Look.

GROUP TECHNOLOGY. The use of a coding and classification system to group products or processes into families with similar attributes.

ICON. A picture or symbol. For instance, a word processing software application might be represented by a symbol for a typewriter.

IMPLOSION. Where detailed data are collected into higher-level summary data. The reverse of explosion.

INDEPENDENT DEMAND. Demand unrelated to the demand for other items, such as space parts demand (Total demand can include both dependent and independent demand.)

INDIVIDUAL JOB ORDER. A requirement to produce a speccificc number of products in any given time period, often tied to a specific customer order or product configuration.

INFINITE CAPACITY PLANNING. Loading a work center or plant without regard to its capacity. Used to show where overloads exist so they can be corrected by planner intervention.

INTEGRATED. Having a seamless characteristic throughout the entire process or picture. With regard to computer systems, this also implies working with the sparsest possible set of data, i.e., no data redundancy.

INTERNAL MEMORY. The random access memory (RAM) of a computer's central processing unit (CPU), as opposed to external memory typified by disk or tape devices.

INVENTORY BUFFER. A pool of inventory that decouples two processes or activities in manufacturing or distribution.

INVENTORY TURNS. How often in a period of time the inventory "turns over" or is used, calculated by dividing sales at cost by the average inventory dollar amount.

JOB SHOP MANUFACTURING. A manufacturing environment where every routing is variable, that is, every product can go through a different sequence of production. Such environments usually have individual shop or job orders, and are likely to have relatively low production volumes, often one unit per product.

JUST-IN-TIME (JIT). A manufacturing philosophy developed by the Japanese that seeks to eliminate all waste in manufacturing business processes.

KANBAN. The information system used to run JIT production. A kanban is a sign that can be as simple as a colored box, a metal tag on a parts container, or a computer-printed bar-coded label or ticket.

LEAD TIME. The amount of time needed for an activity or process to occur.

LINEAR PROGRAMMING MODELS. Computer-based models that solve resource allocation problems with one or more (often hundreds of) constraints.

LOGISTICS. The science that covers the material supply environment, ranging from global suppliers through a manufacturing company's plants through distribution to the final end user.

LOT-FOR-LOT. A lot-sizing algorithm in which the quantity to be produced exactly reflects the amount needed in the time period with no considerations for safety stock or producing any overstock.

LOT SIZE. The quantity of units to be produced in the manufacturing process.

LOT-SIZING ALGORITHM. The algorithm that determines the quantity to be produced after taking into account in a variety of ways supply and demand for a given time period.

MAKE-TO-ORDER. A manufacturing environment where products are only manufactured when a firm customer order is in hand. This may be due to policy, or more often to the fact that each product is custom-specified by a customer at the time of order.

MAKE-TO-STOCK. A manufacturing environment where standard products are produced and often stocked in a distribution network that starts with a finished goods warehouse.

MANUFACTURING RESOURCE PLANNING (MRP). The complete application software that contains modules including forecasting, order entry, master production scheduling, capacity requirements planning, material requirements planning, procurement, shop floor control, and cost accounting. MRP II packages contain integrated accounting and financial reporting functions as well.

MASTER PRODUCTION SCHEDULE (MPS). A statement of the products a manufacturing enterprise will produce in a given time period, after taking into account the products' supply and demand.

MATERIAL REQUIREMENTS PLANNING (mrp). An order-scheduling mechanism that sets and maintains order priorities for manufactured or purchased parts. The basis for scheduling is the explosion or required product quantities (determined by the time-phased master production schedule) through each product's bill of materials to determine gross requirements, and then netting these requirements against parts on hand or due in (scheduled receipts).

MONTE CARLO SAMPLING. A random sampling technique based on known probability functions to obtain a probabilistic solution to a real-world problem.

MOVE TIME. The amount of lead time designed into a planning system to allow for the movement of parts and material from one work center to another.

NET CHANGE. Transaction-driven MRP, where the portion of the production or materials plan updated is only that affected by transactions such as inventory receipts or withdrawals, engineering changes, work completion, and so on.

NETTING ALGORITHM. The algorithm that determines the steps used to aggregate demand and calculate net requirements after considering available supply.

OBJECT ORIENTED (OO). A form of software engineering in which objects are formed as abstractions of real-world items that encapsulate a set of variables and methods corresponding to the real-world object's attributes and behaviors. This encapsulation, unlike traditional computing, stores both the computing algorithm *and* its data for the object. Different objects can share commonalities between them through the property of inheritance. Objects can be stored in libraries and selected for linking in a software application program. A major benefit of objects is their reusability.

OPEN SYSTEMS. Computing systems that are not proprietary in design. Open systems are meant to imply interoperability, though this cannot be assumed to be strictly the case today.

OPERATING SYSTEM. The system that coordinates the operation of the essential parts of a computer—CPU, memory devices, internal data management, and so on.

PAST DUE. Parts, material, or work that is late according to its original schedule date.

PEGGING. The ability to work up the product structure to trace the ultimate source of a part's demand all the way to the customer order or forecast originating the part's demand.

PLANNING HORIZON. The amount into the future a given method or system considers when planning—for instance, six months, one year, three years.

PORT. To rewrite software so that it can be shifted from operating on one computer design to another.

PREVENTIVE MAINTENANCE. The maintenance of production machinery according to some fixed schedule, as opposed to only fixing a machine when it breaks.

PRODUCT STRUCTURE. A hierarchical diagram that shows the relationship of all the raw materials, parts, and components that go into a product during its manufacture. This is analogous to an indented bill of materials. A single level bill of materials would simply show all materials and parts and their quantities going into a product without regard for component and subassembly or structural information.

PRODUCT STRUCTURE TAXONOMY. The hierarchy from topmost grouping such as group down to individual stock keeping units at the bottom, for example, group, family, class, style, SKU.

PROPRIETARY. A design that is uniquely one manufacturer's, i.e., not the same as any other manufacturer's.

PULL. Refers to a product or part production that is *only* initiated by demand from a *downstream* activity such as a customer order or order from the next work center in the production process.

PUSH. Refers to a product or parts order initiated by a planning system that orders the production of a quantity of parts without being totally supported by customer orders. Here, downstream work centers have no say in the quantity of parts they produce. The "push" comes from some central management source.

QUEUE TIME. The amount of time a part is waiting in line to be worked on at a work center.

RATE-BASED SCHEDULING. Scheduling a plant or line at a fixed rate basis, such as 400 cases per day or 200 items per shift, as opposed to shop or job orders of varying fixed lot sizes or cum scheduling.

REAL-TIME. As used in this book, activities that take place in minutes, not hours, days, weeks, or months. Not meant in this book to be the same as real-time in process control, where subsecond response times are required.

REDUCED INSTRUCTION SET COMPUTER (RISC). A computer architecture that operates with fewer internal instruction sets than a CISC or conventional instruction set computer. RISC computers generally are much faster that CISC computers for the equivalent sophistication of microprocessor design.

REGENERATIVE. A form of materials planning where, at each run, all the previous plan is thrown away and a completely new plan is developed. This contrasts with net change MRP, where usually only a portion of the old plan is ever discarded.

RELATIONAL (DATABASE MANAGEMENT SYSTEM). A form of database management system design in which data are carried in rows and columns. Unlike conventional hierarchical or network database designs, there is no relationship fixed between data elements. Relationships between data elements are either carried in the data or developed by the inquiry software on the fly when accessing the data.

REPETITIVE MANUFACTURING. A manufacturing environment in which routings are generally fixed (the products go down a line), production schedules are reasonably fixed and rate-based, and the production volumes are medium to high per product.

ROUTING. The series of operations a product will go through to be manufactured.

SAFETY STOCK. The amount of extra inventory carried on hand to account for the uncertainty or variability of demand.

SCRAP FACTOR. The percentage of units added by a lot-sizing algorithm to allow for planned losses due to quality problems in manufacture.

SETUP TIME. The amount of time needed to prepare a work center or machine for operation at production rates and quality levels for a particular part.

SIMULATION. A form of computer modeling that attempts to duplicate some real-world process (generally in abstracted form) and, by varying the model's input, predict the behavior of the system under certain conditions.

SIX SIGMA. A term used as a measure of quality, wherein good parts will represent plus and minus six standard deviations within a normal distribution, and thus bad parts will equal 2.2 per million with no process shift, and 3.4 parts per million with a 1.5 standard deviation process shift.

STOCK KEEPING UNIT (SKU). A part or product kept in stock as a uniquely identified item.

STRUCTURED QUERY LANGUAGE (SQL). A set of standardized calls to elicit data from relational database management systems.

SUPPLY CHAIN. Refers to the logistics chain prior to a particular point. For a manufacturer, supply chain is the total environment from which it sources raw materials and parts.

TIME BUCKETS. The size of the time segments in which a planning system groups events, for example, days, weeks, months, quarters, or years.

TOTAL QUALITY MANAGEMENT (TQM). A complete philosophy of company-wide quality control that includes many lesser-quality tools, such as quality function deployment, Taguchi methods, and statistical quality control, among others, to achieve world-class quality performance.

TOTAL SUPPLY CHAIN. Often used to describe the total logistics environment from global suppliers through manufacturing through distribution to the end user or customer.

VALUE-ADDED PIPELINE. The total logistics environment from global suppliers through manufacturing through distribution to the end user or customer.

VIRTUAL ENTERPRISE. A transient business entity made up of elements of different corporations' business units enabled by modern information systems and telecommunications.

Index

About the Author

Thomas G. Gunn is president of Gunn Associates, Inc. in Bryn Mawr, Pennsylvania. With over fifteen years of management consulting experience in the manufacturing industry, he specializes in assisting manufacturing companies with their development of manufacturing strategies and performance improvement programs to increase their competitive advantage in global markets and significantly move them toward world class business performance. He is a frequent speaker at industry conferences and internal executive education programs sponsored by many companies. He has delivered over 300 executive education speeches and seminars in North America and Europe.

In addition, Mr. Gunn is a well-published author on manufacturing management. His most recent books are *21st Century Manufacturing: Creating Winning Business Performance* (Harper Trade, 1992), and *Manufacturing for Competitive Advantage: Becoming a World Class Manufacturer* (Ballinger, 1986). He has also written extensively for such publications as *Scientific American, Production, Datamation, Managing Automation, CIM Review, OR/MS Today*, and *Chief Executive*.

The author's corporate experience includes: vice president, Distribution and Procurement, UNISYS Corporation; partner and national director, Manufacturing Consulting Group, Arthur Young & Company; and vice president, Computer Integrated Manufacturing Group, Arthur D. Little, Inc. He holds an M.B.A. from the Amos Tuck School at Dartmouth College and a B.S. in mechanical engineering from Northeastern University. He is a certified member of the American Production and Inventory Control Society (APICS) and a member of the Society of Manufacturing Engineers. He is currently serving a three-year membership on the Manufacturing Studies Board of the National Research Council's Commission on Engineering and Technical Systems. In addition, Thomas Gunn teaches at the Wharton School of the University of Pennsylvania in its Executive MBA and Advanced Management Programs.

Recently, Mr. Gunn has become CEO and president of Enterprise Planning Systems, Inc., a manufacturing software and services company with its U.S. headquarters in Lexington, Massachusetts, and world headquarters near Ottawa, Ontario, Canada.